5965

/

TELEPEN

005965

D1099196

YO

Gener...   ...versity
of Stir...   ...can
University of Beirut

John Dryden

SELECTED POEMS

Notes by Christopher S. Nassaar

BA (BEIRUT) MA (SUSSEX) PH D (WISCONSIN)
Associate Professor of English and Cultural Studies,
The American University of Beirut

LONGMAN
YORK PRESS

To the memory of my father, Maurice George Nassaar, MD

ST. HELENS
COLLEGE

821.9
KRIM JEF

E= JUL 1988

LIBRARY

YORK PRESS
Immeuble Esseily, Place Riad Solh, Beirut.

LONGMAN GROUP UK LIMITED
Longman House,
Burnt Mill,
Harlow,
Essex

© Librairie du Liban 1987

*All rights reserved. No part of this publication may be reproduced, stored
in a retrieval system, or transmitted in any form or by any means,
electronic, mechanical, photocopying, recording, or otherwise, without the
prior permission of the copyright owner.*

First published 1988

ISBN 0-582-79294-0

Produced by Longman Group (FE) Ltd
Printed in Hong Kong

Contents

Part 1

Introduction

The life and work of John Dryden

The early years

John Dryden (1631–1700) was not only a poet, but also a playwright, critic and translator of both prose and verse. Samuel Johnson (1709–84), the famous English critic, wrote of him:

> Perhaps no nation ever produced a writer that enriched his language with such variety of models. To him we owe the improvement, perhaps the completion of our metre, the refinement of our language, and much of the correctness of our sentiments . . . What was said of Rome adorned by Augustus may be applied by an easy metaphor to English poetry embellished by Dryden . . . he found it brick, and he left it marble.

Dryden was born on 9 August 1631 into a family which had Puritan sympathies. He was the first of fourteen children—four sons and ten daughters—to be born to Erasmus and Mary Dryden. Unfortunately, not very much is known about his life. A recent critic has observed: 'Given the centuries between them, it is startling that we know so little more about Dryden than we know about Chaucer, but the fact may serve as a reminder that the art of biography has its beginnings only in Dryden's lifetime. The desire to preserve personal documents which is stimulated by a tradition of biography and the subsequent tendency to preserve a poet's papers as national treasures belong substantially to a later generation'.*

What we do know about Dryden is that he was born in Northamptonshire, and that, despite forty years of residence in London, he remained attached to his place of birth and paid regular visits to it. We know very little about his boyhood, but it is certain that he went to Westminster School in London around 1646. Dr Richard Busby was the headmaster there, and Dryden seems to have been one of his favourite pupils. Busby gave Dryden a very thorough grounding in the Greek and Latin languages and their literatures. In

---

*David Wykes, *A Preface to Dryden*, Longman, London, 1977, p. 3.

1650, Dryden went to Trinity College, Cambridge, where he obtained a BA in 1654. Trinity College was willing to offer him a place as a postgraduate student, but by that time his father had died and he left the University for good, possibly for financial reasons.

There has been much speculation about Dryden's possible attachment to the Puritan cause during his youth, but there is little solid evidence to support this idea, though it is true that practically all of Northamptonshire favoured the Puritan revolution in its early stages and that Dryden did write a poem on the death of Oliver Cromwell (1599–1658). All this, however, is of secondary importance. What is significant is that Dryden, after the Restoration in 1660, remained a royalist and a Tory throughout the rest of his life.

Dryden's father died in June 1654, leaving him farmland which provided him, for the rest of his life, with a fairly small but steady income. Throughout his adult life, then, Dryden's financial situation was relatively secure, but not enough to relieve him from the burden of earning a living.

In December 1663 he married Lady Elizabeth Howard, daughter of the Earl of Berkshire, and had three sons by her. Family tradition has it that the marriage was an unhappy one, but there is little evidence to support this. More probably their marriage was a steady, established one, not passionately romantic but not a failure. The Drydens certainly shared a deep love and concern for their children.

Dryden's poetic career began while he was still a schoolboy, with an elegy to Lord Hastings, who had died of smallpox at the age of nineteen. His first mature poem was 'Heroic Stanzas to the Glorious Memory of Cromwell' (1659), which was soon followed by 'Astraea Redux', published in 1660 to celebrate the Restoration of Charles II (1630–85) as monarch. This was the first of a series of public poems celebrating or defending that monarch.

Dryden the playwright

After the Restoration, the theatres were reopened (the Puritans had closed them down as immoral), and Dryden devoted most of his energy to writing plays. In all, he wrote twenty-eight plays (some in collaboration) and contributed greatly to creating the heroic play, a frankly artificial, somewhat operatic form that depended on spectacle and on fierce, witty debates. Some of his best plays are *Tyrannic Love* (1669), *The Conquest of Granada* (1670; a two-part work in ten acts), *Marriage à-la-Mode* (1672), *Aureng-Zebe* (1675), *All for Love* (1677) and *Don Sebastian* (1690).

For ten years, Dryden wrote exclusively for the King's Theatre, but they gradually fell out. *All for Love*, his most popular play and the one that has enjoyed the greatest reputation with posterity, was the last he gave to the King's Theatre. A mediocre production of it in December 1677 failed to make any impact, and this probably helped Dryden to decide to give his future plays to the Duke's Theatre. The writing of plays provided him with an insecure income, and he was eventually happy to renounce the theatre in the late 1670s and to concentrate on other literary activities, although he did make a brief return with *Don Sebastian* and other plays. In 1668, moreover, he published an excellent critical dialogue, *Of Dramatic Poesy: An Essay*.

Dryden the poet

In 1668, Dryden was appointed Poet Laureate, that is, the official poet of the state. By that time, he had published *Annus Mirabilis* (1667) but had not yet written any of the great poems for which he is remembered today. The Laureateship carried with it a small salary of £200 a year, but more importantly, it gave him prestige.

The first of his great poems, *Absalom and Achitophel*, did not appear until 1681. A political poem presented within a biblical framework, it is Dryden's most masterly achievement. It defends Charles II against Whig demands, led by Shaftesbury (1621–83; he is Achitophel in the poem) and the Duke of Monmouth (1649–85; Absalom in the poem), that he should exclude his Roman Catholic brother from succession to the throne.

A year later, *Mac Flecknoe*, which may have been written as early as 1678, was published. The poem is a superb mock-heroic satire, an attack on a second-rate poet, Thomas Shadwell (?1640–92), who often criticised Dryden. Later poems were 'A Song for St Cecilia's Day' (1687) and 'Alexander's Feast' (1697), both celebrating the power of music.

From 1679 onwards, nearly everything Dryden wrote was printed by Jacob Tonson, who became Dryden's lifelong publisher.

Dryden and religion

Two of Dryden's best-known poems, *Religio Laici* (1682) and *The Hind and the Panther* (1687), deal exclusively with religious matters. The first is a Protestant poem, the second a Catholic one, and they reveal Dryden's changing religious attitudes and his conversion to Catholicism.

Religio Laici—the title means a layman's or non-specialist's religion—offers a defence of moderate Christianity. Dryden insists that the Bible is our only door to knowing the true God, and he rejects Deism or Natural Religion. The Deists argued that supernatural revelation was unnecessary, and that it was possible to infer the existence of God rationally from the careful designs of Nature. Dryden also defends the plain meaning of Scripture against those who wish to come up with twisted, forced interpretations, or to turn clarity into obscurity. In all, *Religio Laici* is a strong defence of the Anglican middle way, an attempt to define the limits and right use of reason in religion. It is also a very well-written poem.

Dryden was born into the Church of England and remained a member of it until his conversion to the Roman Catholic faith in 1685 or 1686 (his Puritan family remained within the Established Church in the days of Cromwell). His conversion came soon after the accession of the Catholic James II (1633–1701) to the throne, but was the result of religious conviction, not—as his enemies claimed—of political opportunism. The reasons why he converted to Catholicism are unclear, but throughout his religious life he was searching for a Church with a solid, proven claim to authority in scriptural matters. Protestantism, with its many sects, its refusal to claim infallibility, and its reliance on the individual's conscience, could not provide him with the same unshakable authority as the Roman Catholic Church. It is not surprising, then, that he finally became a Catholic.

The Hind and the Panther is Dryden's basic Catholic poem. A beast fable, it presents the Anglican Church as a Panther and the Catholic Church as a Hind. The Hind is the best, noblest and most beautiful of animals, while the Panther is a poor second to it. In many respects, Dryden's religious beliefs in this poem are quite the opposite of those expressed in *Religio Laici*. He argues that the Catholic Church has the best claim to religious authority because it is the direct descendant of the early Church. He also defends the doctrine of transubstantiation, the belief that during the Mass the bread and wine of the Eucharist are miraculously changed into the body and blood of Christ. The Church of England (the Panther) is presented as hopelessly confused and lost in a maze of contradictions and compromises.

Dryden the translator

Dryden's career as a translator began in 1680 when Tonson published *Ovid's Epistles, Translated by Several Hands*. Two of these epistles were translated wholly by Dryden and a third in collaboration with the Earl of Musgrove. These were followed by translations of Virgil (70–19BC), Theocritus (*c*.308–*c*.240BC), Lucretius (*c*.96–55BC) and Horace (65–8BC).

Dryden's interest in translation grew gradually. After the 'Glorious Revolution' of 1688 and the accession of the anti-Catholic William (1650–1702) and Mary (1662–94) of Orange, he found himself out of favour and no longer able to write public poems: translation and the writing of plays remained open to him, but the former was a much more reliable and lucrative source of income. So Dryden turned his attention mainly to translation, and produced some of the best verse translations in the English language.

He produced an excellent translation of Juvenal (c.AD60–c.140) and a slightly less effective one of Persius (AD34–62) in 1693. He then collaborated in a translation of Plutarch's (c.AD46–c.120) *Lives*. His major undertaking as a translator, however, was *The Works of Virgil*, begun in 1693 and completed and published in 1697. This was a difficult task, but Dryden accomplished it superbly.

In 1700, the year of his death, Dryden published *Fables Ancient and Modern* made up mostly of translations and a modernisation of some of Chaucer's (?1340–1400) poetry.

Dryden the man

Although brilliantly witty and satirical in his writings, Dryden seems to have been a shy man in society, lacking in boldness and ease. In his various prose writings he often refers to this weakness of his. He was unable, it would seem, to reproduce in society the confidence and ease he displayed on paper.

His relationship with his wife was stable but not passionate. But towards their three sons both he and Lady Elizabeth were openly affectionate and highly protective. When Dryden appealed to royal favour it was almost always for the sake of his sons, either to obtain King's Scholarships for them or—in the case of his son John—to gain his admission as a Fellow of Magdalen College, Oxford. This strong concern for the welfare of his children remained with him till the end of his life.

Alexander Pope (1688–1744), the famous eighteenth-century poet, described him as follows: 'Dryden was not a very genteel man. He was intimate with none but poetical men. He was as plump as Mr Pitt, of a fresh colour, and a down look—and not very conversible.'

John Dryden died on 13 May 1700 and was buried in Westminster Abbey.

The influence of Dryden: Neoclassicism in English literature

Dryden's influence on eighteenth-century literature in general, and on Alexander Pope in particular, is so great that many teachers have tended to treat him as an influence rather than as an original talent. This attitude is unjustified. Dryden's literature is excellent in its own right and within its proper seventeenth-century framework. We should not, however, go to the opposite extreme of ignoring his profound influence. Indeed, the modern poet T. S. Eliot (1888–1965) has remarked: 'We cannot fully enjoy or rightly estimate a hundred years of English poetry unless we fully enjoy Dryden'.

It was Dryden who first exemplified the major tenets of the Neoclassical Movement in English literature. The basic features of this movement are:

(1) The use of the Greek and Roman classics as models while adapting them so that they have a contemporary application.
(2) The insistence on the primacy of Reason.
(3) The love of order.
(4) Interest in what is general and universal, not in what is particular and individual.

It is perhaps worth considering these categories in more detail:

(1) The period of the Restoration and early eighteenth century is often called the Augustan age in England, a term that was coined in the period itself. This reflects the idea that the England of that day was comparable in magnificence and civilisation with the Rome of Augustus Caesar (27BC–AD14). In literature, the writers of the Augustan age often rooted their work in the classics. The purpose was not simply to imitate the classics, but to produce literature modelled on them and equal to them in excellence. Dryden's mock-heroic satire *Mac Flecknoe*, for instance, is rooted in the epics of Homer (*c*.ninth century BC) and Virgil. By elevating a second-rate poet, Thomas Shadwell, to the heights of an epic hero—in other words, by placing the mantle of greatness upon a fool—Dryden fully and brilliantly reveals him as ridiculous. The influence of *Mac Flecknoe* on later satires, especially Pope's *The Dunciad*, is beyond question.

(2) Dryden, in his view of poetry, assigned a major role to reason or judgement as a control of the imagination. He rejected the view that poetry is a form of divine madness that tells us nothing true in the strict, scientific sense. Thus his poems are often arguments where

reason plays a central role (although he was fully aware of the limits of reason and referred to himself as a sceptic). *Absalom and Achitophel*, for example, is a defence of monarchy and conservatism against chaos and rebellion. *The Hind and the Panther* is a lengthy debate between the Anglican Church and the Roman Catholic Church about the respective merits of each.

Other major writers of the eighteenth century accepted the view that reason is man's primary faculty. Jonathan Swift (1667–1745) in *Gulliver's Travels* (1726) presents the ideal human being as a completely rational person. Pope and Dr Johnson also considered the importance of reason to be self-evident.

(3) The love of order or ordered liberty is a prominent feature of Neoclassicism, and again we meet it first in Dryden. This love of order can perhaps best be illustrated by the fondness, in the poetry of the period, for the heroic couplet form with its sense of poise and balance. The heroic couplet is a pair of rhyming iambic pentameter lines that often encapsulate a general idea or truth. Here is an example from *Absalom and Achitophel* on the effects of praise on weak, ambitious minds:

> What cannot praise effect in mighty minds
> When flattery soothes and when ambition blinds!

The heroic couplet, of course, was Dryden's favourite medium.

Even in the attitude towards Nature, we can see this pervasive love of order. Rugged landscapes were rejected in favour of ordered, harmonious ones. The following lines from Pope's *Windsor Forest* sum up the taste of the period:

> Here earth and water seem to strive again,
> Not chaos-like together crush'd and bruis'd
> But as the world, harmoniously confused:
> Where order in variety we see,
> And where, though all things differ, all agree.

(4) Dr Johnson, writing in the eighteenth century, described the role of the poet in the following manner:

> The business of the poet is to examine, not the individual, but the species, to remark general propertie and large appearances; he does not number the streaks of the tulip or describe the different shades of the verdure of the forest. He is to exhibit in his portraits of nature such prominent and striking features as to recall the original to every mind.

This interest in general truths is a basic principle of Neoclassicism, and we first discover it fully exemplified in the verse of Dryden. His religious poems, for example, are a search for universal, permanent metaphysical truth. *Absalom and Achitophel* examines the age-old disease of ambition and love of power, and studies the best form of government. 'Alexander's Feast' shows the influence of music not simply on a particular individual, but on all human beings in all ages. Dryden's concern is with the universal and general, not the individual and eccentric.

The reaction against Neoclassicism in England began around the middle of the eighteenth century, but did not reach its full bloom until the end of that century and the beginning of the nineteenth, when Romanticism became the order of the day. The first of the great Romantic poets, William Blake (1757–1827), remarked: 'We do not want either Greek or Roman models if we are but just and true to our own Imaginations'. Wordsworth (1770–1850) in *The Prelude* (1850) called reason a 'false, secondary power', stressed its limitations, and extolled instead the Imagination, which he defined as a power of the mind that can intuitively understand the nature of the universe and recognise it as a harmonious unit. *The Prelude*, moreover, is about the growth of a particular mind—Wordsworth's. In nature, the Romantics were attracted to wild, rugged, uncultivated landscapes, not to the ordered gardens of the Augustan age. Nor did they write in heroic couplets, but preferred freer, less organised verse forms. Dryden and Pope became the whipping boys of the Romantics, their example of bad taste in poetry. Students today have to put aside the prejudices and preoccupations of the Romantics before they can begin to appreciate Dryden.

A note on the text

Absalom and Achitophel was first published in London by Jacob Tonson in 1681. *Mac Flecknoe* was first published in 1682, again by Jacob Tonson in London. 'A Song for St Cecilia's Day' first appeared in 1687, 'Alexander's Feast' in 1697.

James Kinsley's *Poems of John Dryden*, 4 volumes, Clarendon Press, Oxford, 1958, contains nearly all of Dryden's verse. Selections of Dryden's poetry that include the four poems mentioned above are available in various inexpensive paperback editions and anthologies. The edition on which these Notes are based is that published by Penguin Books in their Penguin Poetry Library series.

Part 2

Summaries
of SELECTED POEMS

Absalom and Achitophel

To understand *Absalom and Achitophel*, the student must realise that Dryden roots his story in the biblical events of II Samuel 13–18. In the Bible, King David had an illegitimate son, Absalom, who conspired with a wicked politician, Achitophel, and rebelled against his father. Dryden describes a contemporary political conflict in terms of these biblical characters. To understand the poem, we must keep in mind the following simple equation: King David=Charles II; Absalom=the Duke of Monmouth, Charles's illegitimate son; Achitophel=Shaftesbury, a scheming politician who wanted to make Absalom/Monmouth the king of England after Charles, and thus deny accession to the legitimate heir, Charles's brother James, on the grounds that James was a Roman Catholic. The false accusation of a Popish Plot to assassinate Charles II was used to whip up public feeling against James. Once this equation becomes clear in the student's mind, the poem, which appears forbidding at first, becomes a delight. Other helpful parallels are the following: Israel=England; Jebusites=Catholics; Jews=Protestants; Jerusalem=London.

Lines 1–227: The prologue

These lines constitute the prologue of the poem. They introduce the basic characters—King David, Absalom, Achitophel—and describe the political problem.

Dryden begins by describing the many sexual adventures of King David, in a tone that is witty, satirical, but also forgiving. David, he tells us, God's favourite king, is a vigorous man who has slept with many women and who lives in the days before Christ and before polygamy is declared a sin in Israel. His wife, Queen Michal, is sterile, but his slaves and concubines have borne him many sons and he has 'Scattered his Maker's image through the land'. Of his illegitimate sons, who by law cannot succeed him to the throne, the bravest and most beautiful is Absalom.

Absalom early distinguishes himself both on the battlefield and in love, and David is delighted to see 'His youthful image in his son renewed'. Accordingly, he indulges Absalom a great deal, denies none of his wishes, and gives him the beautiful Annabel for a bride. Absalom's faults and 'warm excesses' are ignored by his father, and even the murder of Amnon, Absalom's half-brother, is declared a 'just revenge'.

David's reign, however, is not to go undisturbed. The Jews, 'a headstrong, moody, murm'ring race', pampered and spoiled by God, impossible to please or to govern, begin to imagine that they lack liberty. Unable to find in history a people more free than themselves, they conclude that only savages who live in woods and caves are truly free. They begin to conspire against David, whom they themselves had proclaimed king 'with a general shout'. But 'the sober part of Israel' knows the value of peace, remembers with horror the Israelites's civil wars, and—aided by the king's mildness—tilts the balance in favour of David. The more rebellious Israelites, however, decide that a plot is necessary to discredit the king:

Plots, true or false, are necessary things
To raise up commonwealths and ruin kings.

It happens that the original inhabitants of Jerusalem were Jebusites, but when the Jews grew strong and flourished, these 'men of Jebus' were treated as God's enemies. Not only were they heavily taxed and forbidden to own land, but their gods were 'disgraced and burnt like common wood'.

This attack on their religious symbols 'set the heathen priesthood in a flame', and they now respond by trying to convert as many Jews as possible to their faith. Rumours of a Jebusite Plot to seize power, and even assassinate the king, fill the nation. The result is that the Jewish factions who dislike King David and wish to control the government use these rumours to achieve their own aims.

The first and worst of these ungrateful men is Achitophel, 'A name to all succeeding Ages cursed'. Dryden describes him as blessed with wealth and honour, but filled with hate and wild ambition. Close to insanity, he is 'Resolved to ruin or to rule the state'. Instead of accepting 'lawful fame and lazy happiness', he uses all his power and trickery to block David's brother from accession to the throne by appealing to the rebellious mood of Jewish mobs. His aim is to have Absalom proclaimed king of Israel so that he can rule through him, for Absalom's power would depend not on legal succession but on the mood of a rebellious mob controlled by Achitophel. His method is to accuse David of being pro-Jebusite or even of being himself a Jebusite.

NOTES AND GLOSSARY:

ere:	before
polygamy:	the practice of having many wives
concubine:	mistress
Michal:	the childless Catherine of Braganza, whom Charles II married in 1662
true succession:	a true heir to the throne
seed:	children
progeny:	offspring, children
Absalon:	Absalom, here James Scott (1649–85), the Duke of Monmouth, illegitimate son of Charles II and a Welsh woman
gust:	zest
conscious destiny:	Monmouth was not destined by law to be king
imperial sway:	the throne
foreign fields:	he fought with the French against the Dutch (1672–3) and with the Dutch against the French (1678)
Whate'er:	whatever
'twas:	it was
Annabel:	Anne, Countess of Buccleuch (1651–1732), a very beautiful and wise woman
forbore:	forbade
construed:	considered
o'er:	over
Amnon:	Monmouth had his troops attack and disfigure a man who had insulted Charles II; in the Old Testament, Absalom arranged the murder of his half-brother in revenge for the rape of his sister, Tamar
specious:	seemingly sound but without real merit
Sion:	stands for London in the poem
sincerely:	completely
proves:	tests
Jews:	they represent Protestants in the poem
pampered:	spoiled
debauched:	debased
nor no:	or any
god-smiths:	a reference to the many sects that arose after the Reformation
Adam-wits:	a reference to Adam as the first human rebel; these 'wits' or self-proclaimed geniuses are following in Adam's footsteps
wanted:	lacked

circumscribed:	controlled
savages:	wild beasts
Saul:	he stands for Oliver Cromwell (1599–1658) in the poem
Ishbosheth:	he represents Cromwell's son Richard (1626–1712) in the poem
forgo:	renounce, reject
Hebron:	this represents Scotland; Charles was crowned king there in 1651, long before he became King of England
humour:	mood
Golden Calf:	in the Old Testament the Israelites created a gold idol and worshipped it while Moses was receiving the Ten Commandments on Mount Sinai
state:	republic, a type of government which Dryden despised
bolts:	arrows
factious:	rebellious, divisive
sober:	mature, balanced
affright:	fear
dishonest:	shameful
careful devil:	the Devil is always ready ('careful') to seduce mankind into the same rebellion
pimps for:	pampers to
good Old Cause:	the Commonwealth
Jerusalem:	represents London in the poem
Jebusites:	they represent Roman Catholics in the poem
chosen people:	Protestants in the poem
burnt like common wood:	church images were savagely destroyed during the Commonwealth
heathen priesthood:	here, Roman Catholic priests
whatsoe'er:	whatsoever
Jewish Rabbins:	in the poem, Church of England priests
espouse:	support, proclaim
Plot:	the Popish Plot
decried:	denounced
winnowed:	sifted
in the mass:	whole
Egyptian:	here French and Roman Catholic
must needs:	must
for worship and for food:	a reference to the Catholic belief that the body and blood of Christ are really present in the bread and wine of Communion

sacrificer's:	priest's
stews:	brothels
Hebrew priests:	here, Church of England clergy
fleece:	income from tithes
God's anointed:	the king
want:	lack
hostile:	excessive
impenitence:	refusal to confess one's sins and receive forgiveness
Achitophel:	he represents Anthony Cooper (1621–83), 1st Earl of Shaftesbury and leader of the rebellion against popery and arbitrary royal power
close:	secret
Sagacious:	wise
wit:	genius
Fretted:	eroded
pigmy-body:	a body too small for the 'fiery soul' within it
o'er-informed:	over-informed; filled to overflowing
tenement of clay:	the body
too nigh:	too near
sure:	surely
near:	closely
bounds:	the bound between genius (wit) and madness
prodigal:	spendthrift
unfeathered, two-legged thing:	a reference to Plato's famous definition of man as a 'featherless biped'
Got:	conceived
huddled:	confused, concealed
anarchy:	primordial disorder, chaos
compass:	achieve
triple bond:	the triple alliance of England, Holland and Sweden against France
foreign yoke:	that of France
affecting:	desiring
ne'er:	never
Abbethdin:	presiding judge of the Jewish civil court
redress:	compensate, bring justice to
gown:	the robe of the judge
rankness:	fertility
cockle:	weeds found in grain fields
wanted:	missed, since David, the composer of the psalms, would have devoted one psalm to Achitophel instead of God
slide, not stand:	take mad risks

manifest of:	showing openly
buckler:	principal figure
skulked:	hid in a cowardly manner
buzzing emissaries:	whispered rumours
jealousies:	suspicion
giddy:	foolish
prime:	the beginning of a new lunar cycle
scribes:	historians
wants:	lacks
his title:	to the throne
dregs:	depths
democracy:	literally, the rule of the people, which Dryden regarded as an unstable and dangerous form of government

Lines 228–490: Absalom's temptation by Achitophel

The evil Achitophel, in order to persuade Absalom to lead the rebellion against King David, appeals to his vanity and ambition. It is Absalom's destiny, he argues, to be Israel's 'second Moses', its Saviour. He is the 'people's prayer', and by refusing to reign he is starving and defrauding them. Achitophel urges him to seize the heaven-sent opportunity before it fades away. David has been disgraced by the Jebusite Plot and has become the object of public scorn. His former popularity is gone, and if he should seek foreign aid in Pharaoh (here, Louis XIV of France), this will only incense the Jews even more against him. Nor will Pharaoh support David, or the royal party accept such support. Absalom, since he has royal blood in his veins and is regarded 'as champion of the public good', is the perfect man to lead Israel. His power will not be based on legitimate succession, but on 'the love of all your native land', which is a more solid base.

Absalom, weak-minded and ambitious, yields to temptation, but remains reluctant. He defends his father's right to govern, for David is 'Good, gracious, just, observant of the laws', mild and merciful. King David has given Absalom everything, moreover—except, alas, succession to the throne. Nevertheless Absalom defends David's brother, the legal successor, who, despite popular opposition, 'Of every royal virtue stands possessed'. Absalom, however, ends his speech by rejecting his mother because she did not have royal blood, and states that his soul was 'made for empire'.

Achitophel, 'hell's dire agent', finding that Absalom is hesitant and open to temptation, renews his appeal. He insists that Absalom's qualities are those of a king, and that David is weak and unwise in his generosity. His plan, he says, is to strip David of non-Jebusite support, drain the treasury, then force the king to declare Absalom his legal successor. Achitophel argues that 'the people have a right supreme/ To make their kings; for kings are made for them'. Absalom's love for his father should not block his attempt to gain control of the state. If David really loved his son, would he have denied him the crown, giving it instead to David's Jebusite brother? Nor is it safe to trust David's brother. Once he becomes king, he will seek to eliminate Absalom, for he is already jealous of him. Absalom, therefore, should exercise the right of self-defence.

Achitophel advises Absalom to take up arms in apparent defence of King David, and to accuse David's brother of plotting to murder the king. Thus Absalom will be able to force David to grant him succession to the throne. And it is probable, Achitophel argues, that David wants to do this, but wishes to be pressured into it. In this matter, the king is like a woman who appears to resist a man's advances, but secretly wishes to be taken. Achitophel urges Absalom to 'Commit a pleasing rape upon the crown'.

This final argument convinces Absalom, for its appeal suits his mild nature best, and he agrees to co-operate with Achitophel and 'head the faction' while they are still enthusiastic.

NOTES AND GLOSSARY:

venom:	poison
Auspicious:	fortunate
royal:	promising kingship
cloudy pillar:	in the Bible, God appeared in a pillar of cloud by day and a pillar of fire by night to guide Moses and the Israelites out of Egypt
second Moses:	saviour, deliverer, as Moses delivered the Jews from their Egyptian bondage
rage:	prophetic excitement
diviner:	prophet
unbespoken:	spontaneous
detain:	postpone
Or:	either
bent:	path, direction
spreads her locks before her:	the locks are to be seized, like opportunity
Gath:	in the Bible, the city where David took refuge from Saul; the reference here is to Brussels, where Charles II was in exile during the period of the Commonwealth
anointing oil:	in the Bible, the prophet Samuel anointed David

	with oil to signify God's choice of David as the future king of Israel
Jordan's sand:	in the Bible, David crossed the river Jordan to resume his kingdom; the reference is to Dover Beach, where Charles II landed in 1660
Prince of Angels:	Satan
sheaf:	bundle
Naked of:	without
Pharaoh's:	the reference is to Louis XIV of France
dissembled:	false
e'er:	ever
'tis:	it is
gaudy:	flashy, brilliantly showy but not in good taste
successive title:	a title based on legitimate succession
mouldy:	decayed and crumbling
Noah's ark:	a reference to the theory that Noah was the first king
effect:	produce
angel's metal:	gold coins; the ambition (mettle) that led the dark angels to rebel
debauched:	debased, spoiled
loath:	reluctant
wonders:	heavenly signs of favour
espoused:	championed
sues:	appeals
yoke:	enslave
dog-star:	the star Sirius, thought to cause madness
nature's holy bands:	the bond of kinship; Absalom is David's son
Prevents:	anticipates
diadem:	crown
augment:	increase
collat'ral line:	the nearest legitimate king, that is, Charles's brother James
oppressed with vulgar spite:	opposed because he is a Roman Catholic
kind:	family, nature
repine:	complain
propitiously:	favourably
scanted:	thwarted
niggard:	low
disclaims:	rejects
staggering:	hesitating
hell's dire agent:	Achitophel
contemn:	condemn
becomes:	befits

Sanhedrin:	the supreme council of the Jews; in the poem, Parliament
shekel:	penny
prerogative:	the powers of the king which were uncircumscribed by law and which Parliament sought to limit by controlling his finances
ply:	worry
obnoxious:	disgusting, repulsive
elders:	rulers; that is, Parliament
right:	James's right to succeed Charles
doubtful:	unlawful
God was their king:	the Commonwealth acknowledged only God as king
durst:	dared
propagate:	perpetuate, ensure the everlastingness of
Or let:	either let
alienate:	give the title to another person
a legacy of barren land:	the Border estate of Monmouth's wife
lays:	the Psalms of David
dissembling:	pretending
Constrains:	controls
contracts:	withdraws
at the last:	in the end
vulgar:	common people
expedients:	solutions
afford:	accept, tolerate
warm:	impulsive
plighted:	pledged
constrained:	forced, raped
affects the frown:	pretends to be angry
blandishments:	words of flattery
popularly prosecute:	lead the majority's movement against

Lines 491–681: The gallery of fools

To strengthen the rebellion, Achitophel unites all the malcontents of Israel. Dryden uses all his wit and satire to discredit this incredible group. He dissects them at length, exposing them as foolish, greedy, envious, selfish, or simply evil.

The best of them are seen as mistaken men, patriots who think that the power of the monarch is too great and wish to limit it. Next there are people who consider only their self-interest, and wish to embroil the state so they can 'sell their duty at a dearer rate'. Others want to abolish monarchy as an institution because they find it useless and expensive. Still others, doubly dangerous, want to abolish monarchy and institute a republic. These are the London rabble, treasonable by nature and led by fanatical priests whose aim is to establish a theocracy, a rule of the priesthood. The most numerous group, however, is 'the herd', common people 'Who think too little and who talk too much'. This group hates Jebusites by instinct, and follows any anti-Jebusite politician.

Some of the chiefs of this rebellion are 'princes of the land'. Foremost among them is Zimri, a very inconstant man, 'Stiff in opinions, always in the wrong', as changeable as the moon: so extreme that every man with him is either a god or a devil. It is his peculiar art to squander wealth, and fools have robbed him of his estate. Laughed out of court, he consoles himself by forming political parties, but never manages to become the leader of any. Thus it is that he is forced to follow Absalom and Achitophel instead of leading the rebellion himself.

It would be tedious, Dryden tells us, to list all the other names involved against King David. Shimei, however, 'who Heaven's anointed dared to curse', must be described. A supposedly religious republican bitterly opposed to the king, he never breaks the Sabbath 'but for gain'. Nor does he ever curse anyone—except the government. Because of the wealth he has amassed, the city has chosen him to be a magistrate. As judge, he pardons all offences against the king:

For laws are only made to punish those
Who serve the King, and to protect his foes.

He never drinks, and eats so little that his cooks have forgotten their trade. Although his kitchen is cool, however, his brains are 'hot'. Ascetic and frugal, he concentrates all his zeal against kingship.

Corah is a third person who should be mentioned, Dryden says. Shameless and serpent-like, he has sunken eyes and a harsh, loud voice. His basic feature, though, is an incredible memory that he can draw on to accuse others of plots 'exceeding man's belief'. Corah's lies are so ingenious that they cannot be called lies in the strict sense of the word, 'For human wit could never such devise'. His evidence concerning a Jebusite Plot is wondrously suited to the temper of the times, and is the 'best that could be had for love or coin'.

NOTES AND GLOSSARY:

for interest: for their private interests
embroil: plunge into trouble
dearer: more expensive

an:	a
husbandry:	thrift
haranguers:	worriers, critics, persecutors
preferment:	advancement
the King:	monarchy
Solymaean rout:	London rabble; Solyma is another name for Jerusalem
Ethnick:	Popish, or Gentile
Hot Levites:	here, the Presbyterian clergy
pulled before/ From th' Ark:	the Presbyterian clergy were deprived of church livings by the Act of Uniformity (1662); the Ark is the Established or State Church
the Judge's days:	representing here the Commonwealth
bore:	governed
cant:	slogans, jargon
zealous:	fanatical
theocracy:	rule of the clergy
Sanhedrin:	here, Parliament
who so fit for reign:	who is so fit to rule
Aaron's race:	the priesthood
found:	establish
grace:	in purity of faith or God's election rather than natural or civil law
deepest mouthed:	baying most loudly in the pack of hunting dogs
dreaming saints:	here, radical Protestants, visionaries
enthusiastic:	inspired
'Gainst:	against
in their own despite:	despite themselves; that is, they are predestined to be saved
hydra:	a mythical many-headed monster; when one or more of its heads were cut off, it grew new ones
score:	enumerate
Zimri:	here, George Villiers (1628–87), second Duke of Buckingham and author of the play *The Rehearsal*, which mocked Dryden; an active opponent of Charles II
epitome:	summary, typical example
chemist:	alchemist
buffoon:	fool, clown
freaks:	whims
employ:	employ himself
Railing:	attacking, criticising
desert:	correct, rewardable behaviour

Beggared:	turned into a beggar
found:	found out
spite of him:	in spite of him
bereft:	deprived
faction:	strife, rebellion
'twere:	it were
well-hung:	suggesting either verbal fluency or sexual vigour
Balaam:	here, most probably, Theophilus Hastings (1650–1701), 7th Earl of Huntington
Caleb:	here, Arthur Capel (1632–83), Earl of Essex
canting:	constantly railing and verbally attacking
Nadab:	here, Lord Howard of Escrick (1626–94), formerly an Anabaptist preacher who railed against the king
new porridge:	revised the Anglican service
Paschal Lamb:	Christ
bull-faced Jonas:	here, Sir William Jones (1631–82), attorney general and prosecutor in the Popish Plot trials; he helped to draft legislation to exclude James from the throne
Shimei:	here, Slingsby Bethel (1617–97), one of the two Whig sheriffs of London and a republican bitterly opposed to Charles; in the Bible, the loyal supporter of Saul who stones and curses David
but for gain:	except for profit; a reference to Puritan thrift, presented here as hypocritical miserliness
vare:	staff
Belial:	one of the dark angels that fell with Satan; here, wickedness
pelf:	stolen goods
wicked neighbour:	a reversal of Jesus's teaching; instead of charity, Shimei supports complicity in crime
durst:	dared
by writing:	writing pamphlets such as *The Interest of Princes and States* (1680)
clog:	impediment, block
that:	so that
Rechabite:	a member of a sect which had sworn never to drink any wine
shrieval:	sheriff's
City feast:	lavish hospitality, which was expected of a sheriff. Bethel was notorious for his meanness in such matters, and especially for his refusal in 1680 to

provide the customary dinner given to aldermen when sheriffs were sworn in

sure: surely

towns once burnt: a reference to the great fire of London (1666), popularly interpreted as divine punishment

spiritual food: Communion; here a miser's substitute for home cooking

Mount: Mount Sinai, where Moses received the Ten Commandments

speak: enumerate

well-breathed: long-winded

Corah: here, Titus Oates (1649–1705), a Roman Catholic priest who turned against the Catholics and became the chief witness of the Popish Plot

pass: be excluded

Brass: an impenetrable metal; the suggestion is that Oates is shameless or insensible

Serpent: a reference to the serpent of brass that Moses made to cure his people of the bites of fiery serpents (see the Bible, Numbers 21: 6–9)

weaver's issue: Oates was the son of a weaver

witnesses' high race: the early Christians

Stephen: the first martyr of the Christian church; false witnesses testified against him and he was stoned to death

Ours: our false witness; that is, Oates

choleric: bad tempered

church vermilion and a Moses' face: the red, well-fed look of a clergyman, the ironic counterpart of the shining face of Moses on his descent from Mount Sinai (see the Bible, Exodus 34:29)

prophet: Oates kept recalling events he claimed to have forgotten in earlier testimony

Rabbinical degree: a degree in divinity

foreign university: the University of Salamanca; Oates claimed to have received a degree in divinity from there, but this was denied by the university

apocryphal: doubtful in authenticity

forfeits: fines

dire: causing or attended with great fear or suffering

whet: sharpen

latitude: freedom to act

Agag: here, Lord Stafford, executed on Oates's evidence in 1680. In the Old Testament, the prophet Samuel harshly ordered Saul to execute Agag, his captured enemy, for God had so commanded

coin: money

Lines 682–752: The fallen Absalom's rebellious speech to Israel

---

Surrounded with such friends, Absalom leaves the court and leads the rebellion. He easily captures the admiration of the crowd and 'glides unfelt into their secret hearts'. He makes a short but highly effective speech to them.

Absalom informs the Israelites that he mourns for them and that he is being persecuted by King David for their sake. Egypt and Tyrus are threatening the trade of Israel, and the Jebusites are seeking to overthrow its religion. King David, the only person who can save Israel, has become his own worst enemy, and 'Exalts his enemies, his friends destroys'. Absalom declares that he loves his father and wishes him no harm. It is not because Absalom wants the crown for himself that he has rebelled—although he believes that the crown is rightfully his—but because he wants to help David and to save Israel.

The listening crowd gives Absalom its full support, and he begins a journey through Israel to gain as much public support as possible. Wherever he goes, he is greeted as a 'young Messiah', a 'guardian god'. He is accompanied, however, by a court formed by Achitophel. Its purpose is to discover the extent of public approval for the rebellion, and to distinguish friends from foes in preparation for battle.

NOTES AND GLOSSARY:

goodly: handsome, attractive

compassionating: bringing compassion upon himself

bespeaking: soliciting

Hybla drops: drops of honey from Hybla in Sicily (Hybla was famous for its honey)

banished man: Monmouth was banished in September 1679, but returned a couple of months later without Charles's permission and received a hero's welcome

arbitrary: unjust

Egypt and Tyrus: here, France and Holland

Bathsheba's: here, a reference to Louise de Kéroualle, the Duchess of Portsmouth and Charles's mistress; in the Old Testament, David committed adultery with Bathsheba

progress:	Monmouth journeyed in 1680 from London to the west of England in a bid for popular support
consecrates:	declares sacred
Issachar:	here, Thomas Thynne (1648–82), a supporter of Monmouth
fathom:	measure
try:	test
specious:	seemingly sound but without any real merit
wife:	Oates accused the queen of being involved in a plot to poison the king
pageant show:	colourful exhibition

Lines 753–810: Dryden speaks out against revolution

Dryden attacks the Israelites for not learning from the past, and for continuing to make the same mistakes. Kings are not 'officers in trust', he argues, who can be judged and removed by crowds. Kingship is a sacred institution traceable to Adam. Kings are not 'slaves to those whom they command'. They rule by divine decree, and the succession of one king by another is bound by divine and human laws. Any attempt to depose a king or to break the line of succession will in the end destroy government itself, and people will find themselves in a state of nature, where the only law is that of the jungle.

This does not mean, of course, that monarchs do not make mistakes, says Dryden. They do, and in such cases it is the duty of the public to correct those errors—'To patch the flaws and buttress up the wall'—so that the ark of the state may remain strong and unshakable. But to revolt against the king is to sink the ark, to ruin the whole through trying to mend the parts. Such behaviour breaks both 'divine and human laws', and is a terrible curse that this 'tamp'ring world' is subject to.

NOTES AND GLOSSARY:

circumvented:	trapped, tricked
contingent:	possible
unbounded arbitrary lord:	a lord who knows no borders or justice
officers in trust:	that is, kings rule by a contract whereby the people give them power
resuming cov'nant:	agreement that the people can resume their power whenever they please to decide who will succeed the current king.
gave the sceptre:	the people who made the original covenant that established monarchy
forfeit on mankind:	a reference to the fact that we are all sinners

ST. HELENS COLLEGE LIBRARY
WATER STREET, ST. HELENS WA10 1PZ
0744 33766 EXT: 225

because of Adam's original sin; that is, Adam
betrayed all mankind

tenants: on lease
for property allowed: taken to be the people's property
fickle rout: moody, changeable crowd or rabble
flowing to the mark, runs faster out: the higher the tide, the faster
it runs out; the moon, the source of lunacy, is
responsible for the movement of the tides
Sanhedrins: here, members of Parliament
whene'er: whenever
nature's state: the state of nature, described by Hobbes as a
condition of 'war of every man against every man'
and where power is the only law. Dryden had
Hobbes specifically in mind here
grant: suppose
but: only
innovation: revolution, starting afresh
buttress up: strengthen
fix the mark: draw the line
touch our Ark: commit sacrilege by destroying the Ark of the
Covenant
base: low
control: break
physic: treat with medicine

Lines 811–932: The friends of King David

The madness of rebellion grows so high that King David finds very
few friends left around him. But some, to their great credit, do
remain. Dryden names them, 'and naming is to praise'.

First on the list is Barzillai, who has a strong history of fighting
rebels. He has a large amount of wealth, but his heart is larger and
knows well how to choose 'the noblest objects'. His eldest son, 'with
every grace adorned', will always be mourned by Dryden. He died
young, but not before achieving the goal of honour. He fought and
defeated both the Tyrians and Egyptians, thus defending his king
with great valour. But Israel was unworthy of him, so Heaven took
him. Dryden hopes that Barzillai's son, as a disencumbered spirit,
will aid the guardian angel of King David. But here Dryden stops,
apologises to Barzillai that his Muse can sing no more about this
painful subject, and turns to other, if lesser, friends of the king.

Zadoc and 'the Sagan of Jerusalem', both holy men, Dryden tells
us, place their resources at King David's disposal, and stimulate the
minds of the people to 'learning and to loyalty'. Adriel, a sharp

judge of good poetry and a friend of poets, defends David in debate and is much loved by him. 'Jotham of piercing wit and pregnant thought', after some faltering, chooses the king's side, and by doing so turns the balance in favour of David, 'So much the weight of one brave man can do'. Dryden then describes Hushai who manages the finances of the state and supplies the 'wanting throne' with 'frugal care'. Finally, there is the noble Amiel, chief of the Sanhedrin, who guides their reason and cools their passion. The Sanhedrin, a parliament representing the tribes of Israel, is divided on the issue of King David's succession, but Amiel defends the crown with great dexterity.

This 'small but faithful band' of worthy people dares to stand by King David and face 'th' united fury of the land'. They recognise the true aim of the revolution, and warn the king that concessions are useless. Absalom wants to snatch the crown from the true successor, while Achitophel is using the Jebusite Plot to ruin the church and the state.

NOTES AND GLOSSARY:

Barzillai: here, James Butler (1610–88), Duke of Ormonde, a strong supporter of Charles II and Royalism; in the Old Testament, Barzillai is an aged benefactor of David

regions waste: here, Ireland, where Ormonde had fought for Charles I

buoy: support

muse: in classical mythology, the Muses were nine sister goddesses who presided over poetry and song; more generally, the goddess or the power regarded as inspiring a poet

more than half a father's name is lost: six of Ormonde's ten children died

eldest hope: Thomas, Earl of Ossory (1634–80), who distinguished himself in battle in support of the Dutch and against the French; died of a fever

unequal: unfair

providence's crime: fever

Scanted: limited, circumscribed

infused: poured into others, penetrating others

Tyrians: here, Dutch

Pharaoh: here, France

durst: dared

disencumbered: freed from the cumbersome body

thence: there

thy:	your
mayst:	may
thou:	you
pinions:	small wings
thou canst:	you can
hearse:	the structure over a bier where verse tributes were hung
steepy:	steep
he:	complete man
Zadoc:	here, William Sancroft (1617–93), Archbishop of Canterbury
lowly:	humble

Sagan of Jerusalem: here, Henry Compton (1632–1713), Bishop of London

noble stem: noble descent; Compton was the son of the Earl of Southampton

Him of the western dome: here, John Dolben (1625–86), Dean of Westminster

weighty sense:	great intelligence
prophet's sons:	boys of Westminster School
Next them:	Next after them
Adriel:	here, John Sheffield (1648–1721), Earl of Mulgrave and patron of Dryden's poetry (thus, 'the muses' friend')
Sanhedrin's:	Parliament's
a muse:	an inspiration
disobedient son:	Monmouth
Jotham:	here, George Savile (1633–95), Marquis of Halifax; he defended James II's succession in the Parliamentary debate of 1680 and countered Shaftesbury's eloquence with an even greater eloquence, thus swaying Parliament to support Charles II
pregnant:	fruitful
Hushai:	here, Laurence Hyde (1642–1711), an ardent royalist and patron of Dryden
foreign treaties:	Hyde negotiated the Anglo-Dutch alliance of 1678
wanting:	lacking money
Amiel:	here, Edward Seymour (1633–1708), Speaker of the House of Commons
dext'rous:	skilful

unequal ruler of the day: in classical mythology Phaeton, Apollo's son, attempted to drive his father's sun chariot

	across the sky but lost control, upsetting the climate and seasons
Sabbath:	leisure
in the breach:	against the popular current
plume:	pluck away
lenitives:	pain killers
fomented:	increased
pernicious:	dangerous

Lines 933–1031: King David invokes the law and restores order

Finally King David, his patience tired, speaks with godlike majesty and heavenly inspiration, and his subjects discern God's voice through that of their king.

So far, David says, his natural tendency to mercy and his love of Absalom have delayed his revenge, but the offenders have gone too far. They have questioned his right to rule and have tried to impose their will on him. He compares Absalom to a 'young Samson' who wants to bring the pillars of the state down on everyone. King David loves Absalom, but Absalom has not been ordained by God to be the next king, and no one has the right to brush aside the law and impose an heir to the throne, least of all a band of rebels. Besides, if the people choose a future king without David's permission, this infers that they have a right to depose the present king.

King David then makes a solid and unalterable decision:

The law shall still direct my peaceful sway,
And the same law teach rebels to obey.

David rejects arbitrary power in the hands of Parliament and the people. He is the king; it is his duty to rule and save the people, even if he has to draw the sword of justice and punish offenders. Naturally merciful, he hates the task of exacting punishment, but he must in order to uphold the law. The rebellion is ugly and viper-like, and the rebels plot not only against him but also against each other. But factious crowds express 'all their brutal rage' at the outset, then 'stand all breathless'. At first, one should avoid them, and strike only after their power has been exhausted. David has no doubt that lawful power will defeat rebel factions in the end.

As King David speaks, the Almighty gives his approval with peals of thunder that shake the firmament. A new age begins, of long duration.

Once more the god-like David was restored,
And willing nations knew their lawful lord.

NOTES AND GLOSSARY:

careful:	troubled
event:	development
train:	subjects
dissembled:	concealed
assuage:	to make milder or less severe
clemency:	mercy, leniency
affronts:	insults
my young Samson:	here, Monmouth; in the Old Testament Samson brought down the house of the Philistines and died in its ruins
Gulled:	fooled, duped
brave:	champion
Whence:	from where
instructor:	Achitophel
give their own:	that is, give what is in their power to give
requisite:	necessary
Esau's hands suit ill with Jacob's voice:	the reference is to deception. In the Old Testament, Jacob deceived his blind father and won a blessing intended for his brother Esau; unable to disguise his voice, Jacob disguised his hands, making them feel hairy, like Esau's, and thus fooled his father
Unsatiate:	having a hunger that cannot be satisfied
control:	contravene
pow'r to punish ere they prove:	arbitrary power
ill:	poorly
grace:	mercy, with divine implications
hinder parts:	back parts, as opposed to the 'front'; in the Old Testament, God warns Moses that no man can see His face and live: 'thou shalt see my back parts; but my face shall not be seen' (Exodus 33: 23)
dire:	causing great fear or suffering
artificers:	craftsmen
viper-like:	snake-like
nutriment:	nourishment
principle of life before:	the reference is to Edmund Spenser's *The Faerie Queene* (I. i. 25), where the offspring of the dragon Error suck up their dying mother's blood, 'Making her death their life'
Belial:	one of the dark angels that fell with Satan
Belzebub:	Beelzebub, another of the dark angels that fell with Satan

event: outcome
factious: rebellious
Then: at this point
'em: them
traverse: oppose
delude: trick
said: spoke
firmament: sky
series of new time: new age

Mac Flecknoe

The title of the poem means 'son of Flecknoe'. Richard Flecknoe (d. 1678) was a notoriously bad Irish poet. In this mock-heroic satire, Dryden has him choose a successor in Thomas Shadwell. Shadwell considered himself the true heir of the great Ben Jonson (1572–1637), and felt that Dryden's admiration of Jonson was less than complete. For over ten years, Shadwell and Dryden engaged in critical disputes, but without any great animosity. Dryden probably wrote *Mac Flecknoe* after being angered by Shadwell's praise of Buckingham's play *The Rehearsal* (1671), in which Dryden's heroic tragedies were ridiculed.

Mac Flecknoe is full of allusions to literary figures, plays, poems, publishers, and so on. Inevitably, the student will find this an obstacle to the enjoyment of the poem. Constant references to the glossary are therefore necessary, and the poem should be read more than once. Once the allusions are understood, the poem becomes extremely enjoyable.

The usual practice in Dryden's day was never to use a living person's full name in a satire, so, in early editions, Shadwell is referred to throughout as Sh—, and this is the form used in these Notes.

Lines 1–63: Flecknoe's first speech in praise of Sh—

Since all human things ultimately decay, Dryden tells us, even Flecknoe, the undisputed emperor of nonsense in prose and verse since his youth, finally grows old. Blessed with many children, he decides to choose one of them to be crowned as his successor 'and wage immortal war with wit'. The choice is easy, for Sh— is clearly the dullest and most stupid of his offspring.

Flecknoe praises Sh— without reserve as 'confirmed in full stupidity' and 'Mature in dullness from his tender years', fat and empty-headed:

The rest to some faint meaning make pretence,
But Sh— never deviates into sense.

Literary figures like Heywood and Shirley merely foreshadowed him, for Sh— is the 'last great prophet of tautology'. Flecknoe declares that even he, 'a dunce of more renown than they', was merely sent 'to prepare thy way'. His 'warbling lute', when he sang to King John of Portugal, was but a prelude to that great day when Sh— sailed on the Thames and sang. Flecknoe compares his favourite son to 'a new Arion':

About thy boat the little fishes throng
As at the morning toast that floats along.

Sh—'s ridiculous music attracts people from 'Pissing-Alley', exceeds St Andre's flat-footed verse in awfulness, and—declares Flecknoe jubilantly—has made Singleton swear that he will never again act the role of Villerius.

Flecknoe ends his speech here, and weeps for joy. Everything, 'but most [of all] his plays', indicates that Sh— was made for 'anointed dullness'.

NOTES AND GLOSSARY:

Flecknoe: Richard Flecknoe (d. 1678), a notoriously bad Irish poet

Augustus: Octavius Caesar, the first emperor of Rome; he became emperor in 31BC, at the age of 32, assumed the title of Augustus four years later, and ruled for 45 years

owned: acknowledged

issue of a large increase: many children

debate: decide

Sh—: Thomas Shadwell (?1640–92), a minor poet and playwright who became engaged in a long public dispute with Dryden on such matters as the nature of wit

goodly fabric: a reference to Shadwell's fat body

thoughtless: mindless

supinely: listlessly, inactively

Heywood and Shirley: Thomas Heywood (?1574–1641) and James Shirley (1596–1666), both popular dramatists who wrote a large number of plays; they were out of favour in Dryden's day

types: foreshadowings, just like David, Solomon and the prophets in the Old Testament, all of whom foreshadow Christ, who is the culmination

tautology:	needless repetition
dunce:	idiot, fool
prepare thy way:	as John the Baptist prepared the way for Jesus
Norwich drugget:	a coarse fabric of wool and linen (Shadwell was from Norfolk)
warbling lute:	Flecknoe had musical pretensions, and was made fun of by many people for this
whilom:	formerly
King John of Portugal:	Flecknoe had visited Portugal and claimed to have received the admiration and patronage of its king
thou:	you
Thames:	the river Thames
did'st:	did
thy:	your
ne'er:	never
Epsom:	a reference to Shadwell's comedy *Epsom Wells* (1672)
blankets tossed:	Sir William Hearty, in Shadwell's play *The Virtuoso* (1676), is a self-styled wit who is tossed in blankets
Arion:	a legendary Greek musician who charmed a group of dolphins with his music and thus saved himself from drowning
treble:	a shrill, high-pitched musical sound
basses:	a very low-pitched musical sound
Pissing-Alley:	the place actually exists and is the name of five streets, one of them near the Thames
Aston Hall:	an unidentified place, but presumably familiar in Dryden's day
About:	around
morning toast:	sewage, garbage and faeces
Thou wield'st:	you wield
threshing:	the act of removing grain from wheat
St Andre's:	a reference to the French dancing master who writes flat-footed verse in Shadwell's opera *Psyche* (1675)
number:	metre
Singleton:	John Singleton, a royal musician
forswore:	rejected forever
Villerius:	a character in Sir William Davenant's *Siege of Rhodes* (1656), a play often ridiculed for sacrificing sense to sound by presenting battles in

recitative, requiring the actor to use both 'lute and sword'

more:	again
most:	most of all
anointed:	crowned

Lines 64–133: The coronation of Sh—

Close to the walls surrounding the fair city of Augusta (a city 'much to fears inclined'), there stands a large building, once a watchtower but now a ruin. 'From its old ruins brothel-houses rise', full of prostitutes and polluted joys. Nearby, a mediocre training school for actors raises its head. The great Fletcher and greater Jonson never appear there, but Simkin, a typical clown in farces, and Panton, another farce character, are very much at home in it.

It is this training school that Flecknoe chooses for the coronation of Sh—, for 'ancient Decker' once prophesied that a mighty prince would rule in this area, a true master of dullness 'Born for a scourge of wit and flail of sense'.

The news of Sh—'s coronation spreads through the city, and people flock to the site from near and far:

No Persian carpets spread th' imperial way,
But scattered limbs of mangled poets lay;

Neglected authors like Heywood, Shirley and Ogilby, whose unsold books gather dust in bookshops, all come to the coronation. Cheated publishers stand as yeomen, with Herringman as captain of the guard.

Finally Flecknoe appears, seated on a throne of his own books. To his right sits Sh—, who is compared to Ascanius, Aeneas's son and 'Rome's other hope', but also to Hannibal, Rome's sworn foe and most dangerous enemy. Like Hannibal, whose father made him swear enmity to Rome, Sh— swears to Flecknoe that he will maintain true dullness till death and will wage constant war against wit and sense.

Flecknoe himself prepares the sacred oil for Sh—'s anointment. He then places a mug of ale in Sh—'s left hand, instead of the orb which the British monarch holds. Instead of a sceptre, he places in Sh—'s right hand a copy of the play *Love's Kingdom*, a pastoral tragi-comedy written by Flecknoe. His temples, finally, are decorated with poppies, to indicate his sleep-inducing dullness. At that exact moment, if fame tells the truth, twelve owls (here symbols of solemn stupidity) fly over Sh—'s left hand, as happened to Romulus, founder and first ruler of Rome, who took 'Presage of sway' from twelve vultures. Sh—'s coronation is cheered by the admiring crowd.

NOTES AND GLOSSARY:

Augusta:	London
fabric:	building
of yore:	in the past
Barbican:	so named because of its former function as an outer defence of the city
hight:	was called
pile:	large building
mother-strumpets:	female owners of houses of prostitution
watch:	the law, constables
Nursery:	a training school for actors
unfledged:	new, untrained
punks:	prostitutes
Maximins:	a reference to the Roman emperor in Dryden's play *Tyrannic Love* (1669); Maximin was a cruel tyrant who raved and ranted and exalted himself a great deal
Fletcher:	John Fletcher (1579–1625), author of many celebrated tragedies in collaboration with Francis Beaumont (1584–1616)
buskins:	the thick-soled boots worn by Greek tragic actors
Jonson:	Ben Jonson (1572–1637), here referred to as a writer of comedy
socks:	the light shoes worn by Greek comic actors (in contrast to 'buskins')
Simkin:	a typical clown in farces
vanished minds:	dead and forgotten authors
clinches:	puns
muse:	in classical mythology, the Muses were nine sister goddesses who presided over poetry and song; more generally, the goddess or the power regarded as inspiring a poet
affords:	offers
Panton:	another farce character, somewhat like Simkin
Decker:	Thomas Dekker (?1572–1632), a fairly able playwright but satirised by Ben Jonson and held in low esteem by Dryden; here presented as a mock-epic counterpart of an Old Testament prophet
Psyches:	a reference to Shadwell's opera *Psyche* (1675)
Misers:	Shadwell's play *The Miser* was published in 1672

Humorists and hypocrites: referring to Shadwell's early unpublished play *Hypocrite; the Humorists*

Raymond: a witty character in *The Humorists*

Bruce: a character in Shadwell's play *The Virtuoso*

near Bunhill and distant Watling Street: a small area in the commercial centre of London

Martyrs of pies and relics of the bum: the unsold books of these authors provide paper for bakers' pans and for privies (lavatories)

Heywood: Thomas Heywood, referred to earlier in line 29

Shirley: James Shirley, also referred to earlier in line 29

Ogleby: John Ogilby (1600–76), a very mediocre translator of Homer and Virgil who also wrote several epics of his own, all of them feeble

Bilked: cheated

stationers: publishers

Herringman: Henry Herringman, who published the works of both Dryden and Shadwell until 1678

hoary: old

Ascanius: Aeneas's son in Virgil's epic *The Aeneid*; here, the reference is to Shadwell as Flecknoe's son

Rome's other hope: that is, Ascanius; Rome here stands for London

lambent: flickering, playing lightly

Hannibal: the great conqueror who almost captured Rome in 216BC; at the age of nine, Hannibal was forced by his father to swear eternal enmity to Rome

sire: father

unction: oil for ointment

priest by trade: Flecknoe was a Roman Catholic priest

sinister: left

instead of ball: the British monarch holds an orb in the left hand and a sceptre in the right

Love's Kingdom: a 'pastoral tragi-comedy' by Flecknoe, published in 1664

At once: at the same time

righteous lore: correct knowledge

Psyche: Shadwell's opera

poppies: opium, suggesting that Shadwell's plays are sleep-inducing

owls: symbols of seriousness and solemnity, in this case not wise but stupid

Romulus: the legendary founder and first ruler of Rome

Tiber's: the river Tiber, in Italy

twice six vultures: that is, twelve vultures

Lines 134–217: Flecknoe's second speech in praise of Sh—

Flecknoe shakes his locks of hair and fights the desire to make a prophetic speech. Failing, he bursts out, asking Heaven to bless his son and let him reign from Ireland to far Barbadoes, and to stretch his pen beyond *Love's Kingdom*. He addresses Sh—, exhorting him to advance 'Still in new impudence, new ignorance'. Let George Etherege triumph on the stage, says Flecknoe, and succeed with such characters as Dorimant, Loveit, Cully and Cockwood. Sh—'s fools shall stand in his defence, and prove their author's lack of sense.

Flecknoe warns Sh— against imitation, so that his characters may be models of dullness completely of his own making and be recognised as original by future ages. In style, he advises him not to 'labour to be dull', but to trust nature, for dullness comes naturally to Sh—. The deliberately silly rhetoric of Sir Formal (in Shadwell's play *The Virtuoso*) will attend Sh—'s pen, though unsought, and dominate all his writing.

Nor should Sh— in any way try to take Ben Jonson for his master. Flecknoe is his father and true master:

Thou art my blood, where Jonson has no part;
What share have we in nature or in art?

Flecknoe then attacks Jonson for not railing 'at arts he did not understand', for never reaching the excellence of Shadwell's opera *Psyche*, for never being coarse, and for never breaking his promises as a playwright. Jonson, moreover, never borrowed scenes from Fletcher while Sh— steals entire scenes from Etherege. Jonson's work is to Sh—'s as oil is to water. When the two are mixed, oil floats above, water sinks below. The lower province is Sh—'s, 'thy wondrous way'. Sh—'s mind is biased in the direction of dullness, which makes all his writings lean to that side.

Sh—'s huge belly, moreover, should not lead him to compare himself to Jonson, who was also fat. Sh—'s belly indicates an emptiness of sense. Flecknoe compares Sh—'s huge frame to a large wine cask, but this is deceptive, for Sh— has within him only a small amount of wit.

Like Flecknoe's, Sh—'s poetry is feeble. His tragedies make people laugh, his comedies put them to sleep. Though his heart may be full of venom, his satires never bite. Sh—'s genius lies not in sharp satiric verse but in rearranging letters and creating anagrams. It is best that he should leave the writing of plays and find 'Some peaceful province in acrostic land', where he can give full play to his

talents 'And torture one poor word ten thousand ways'. Or Sh—
may wish to write his own songs and sing them.

Flecknoe's last words are scarcely heard, for Bruce and Longville
(two characters in *The Virtuoso*) spring a trapdoor that plunges
the 'yet declaiming' poet downwards. The sinking Flecknoe's robe,
however, is borne upwards by the wind and picked up by Sh—:

> The mantle fell to the young prophet's part,
> With double portion of his father's art.

NOTES AND GLOSSARY:

sire: Flecknoe

honours of his head: his locks of hair

damps: drops of sweat

the raging god: Apollo, the god of prophecy in classical mythology; he possessed his priests and priestesses,
causing them to rage as he did so, and prophesied
through them

from Ireland . . . To far Barbadoes: a huge empire largely of water

Love's Kingdom: Flecknoe's 'pastoral tragi-comedy'

Virtuoso's: Shadwell wrote a play entitled *The Virtuoso*

gentle George: Sir George Etherege (?1635–91), a brilliant comic
playwright of the Restoration period

Dorimant: the rake-hero in *The Man of Mode* (1676), Etherege's best play

Loveit: Dorimant's discarded mistress in the same play

Cully, Cockwood, Fopling: comic fools in three of Etherege's plays

pit: the floor of the theatre; the box was the most
fashionable place to sit, the gallery the least
fashionable, with the pit in between

want: lack

'em: them

Sedley: Sir Charles Sedley (?1638–1701), who wrote a
prologue (and possibly more) to Shadwell's play
Epsom Wells

lard: render fat as a pig

Epsom: a reference to Shadwell's play *Epsom Wells*

thou would'st: you would

cull: pick

Sir Formal's oratory: the rhetoric of a silly orator, Sir Formal Trifle,
in Shadwell's play *The Virtuoso*; Shadwell delib-
erately presents him as a silly, foolish, comic
orator; Dryden suggests that Shadwell by nature
is like Sir Formal

quill:	a feather-pen
northern:	suggesting a freezing northern climate where wit is scarce
arrogating:	invoking
Jonson's:	Ben Jonson, the excellent poet and playwright whom Shadwell tried to imitate
Thou art:	you are
Prince Nicander's:	a character in Shadwell's opera *Psyche*
vein:	manner
Psyche's:	*Psyche*, Shadwell's opera
sold he bargains:	asked a question that might be met with a coarse answer such as 'whip-stitch, kiss my arse'
Promised a play:	Shadwell, in the dedication of *The Virtuoso*, promised his audience a play and scorned 'unnatural farce fools, which some intend for comical'
Fletcher:	John Fletcher, the celebrated Renaissance playwright
purloin:	steal, lift
Eth'rege:	George Etherege, the brilliant Restoration playwright
dost:	do
transfuse:	shift
humours:	in the epilogue to his play *The Humorists*, Shadwell defined a humour as a 'bias of the mind' that inclines it naturally in one direction and makes all its actions flow in that particular direction
bias of thy mind:	humour, natural inclination
mountain belly:	Shadwell was fat
likeness:	to Ben Jonson, who was also fat, this being, Dryden feels, the only resemblance between the two writers
tympany:	windiness that created unnatural swelling, thus, emptiness
tun:	large wine cask
sure:	surely
kilderkin:	a small cask, a quarter of a tun
numbers:	verse
gall:	'poisonous anger
thou sett'st thyself:	you set yourself
felonious:	criminal
venom:	poison
Irish:	an English attitude to Ireland, suggesting

	barbarity and lack of skill, inherited from Flecknoe, who is Irish
keen iambics:	sharp satiric verse
anagram:	rearranging letters to form a new word ('Jane', for instance, is an anagram for 'Jean', since the latter name is a rearrangement of the letters in the first)
Leave:	abandon
acrostic:	a poem, the first letters of whose lines spell a name or word
wings display and altars raise:	in shaped poems like George Herbert's (1593–1633) 'Easter Wings' and 'The Altar', which Dryden regarded as examples of false wit; 'The Altar', for instance, is actually shaped like an altar
Bruce and Longville:	two characters who perform a trapdoor trick on the orator, Sir Formal Trifle, in Shadwell's play *The Virtuoso*
yet:	still
declaiming:	speaking eloquently
bard:	poet
drugget:	a coarse fabric of wool and linen
subterranean:	underground
prophet's part:	Shadwell is compared to the prophet Elisha in the Old Testament, who 'took the mantle of Elijah that fell from him' and became his legitimate heir

'A Song for St Cecilia's Day'

Stanza 1

In this stanza, Dryden expresses the idea that the universe was designed in harmonic intervals. Even when the cosmos was a chaos of 'jarring atoms', at the beginning of time, there existed in this chaos the potential for order. The structure of the universe began from heavenly harmony. The Word—a 'tuneful voice'—commanded the jarring atoms to organise themselves. The four contraries, cold, hot, moist and dry, which make up the four elements, obeyed the power of music and took their assigned positions. They formed a Chain of Being, each creature linked to every other in a necessary sequence.

Creation thus forms the fullest of harmonies, in which all possible notes are heard, and in which the closing note—the 'diapason'—is Man.

Stanza 2
Dryden states that music is capable of raising or calming any passion. He refers to Jubal, who, the Bible tells us, was 'the father of all such as handle the harp and organ' (Genesis 4: 21). Jubal is presented as the first musician. When he played music on a 'corded shell', his brethren gathered around, then fell on their faces to worship that heavenly sound. They were convinced that a god dwelt inside the shell that gave forth such sweet music.

Stanzas 3–6
These stanzas talk about the power of various musical instruments while also demonstrating this power in the poetic rhythm. The trumpet, for instance, excites us to take up arms and go to war, and so does the drum with its 'double double double beat'. The flute, on the other hand, expresses the sorrow and grief of hopeless lovers. The sharp music of the violin is ideal for expressing such emotions as fury, jealousy and indignation. Its music can capture the extremes of pain and passion for a 'fair, disdainful dame'.

Of all the musical instruments, however, the most superior is the organ, for its notes inspire holy love and are more perfect even than the heavenly choirs. The organ's notes move heavenwards and 'mend the choirs above'.

Stanza 7
Dryden begins this stanza with a reference to Orpheus, who represents the power of music in traditional pagan myth. When he played his lyre, beasts followed him and trees uprooted themselves to go after him. But Cecilia performed an even greater miracle with music. When she played her organ fitted with pipes, an angel heard the music and appeared, mistaking earth for heaven.

Grand Chorus
The chorus states that music is the very heart of the cosmos. It was sacred music that first brought form and order to the universe. The result was the music of the spheres, which constantly sings the praise of God. Also, when Judgement Day comes and the cosmos is devoured, this shall be done through the music of a heavenly trumpet.

NOTES AND GLOSSARY:
St Cecilia's Day: 22 November; St Cecilia was the patroness of music and it was the custom in Dryden's time for distinguished poets to write annual odes in celebration of her

This universal frame: the structure of the universe

nature: the physical world, sunk in primal chaos but containing the potential of becoming ordered

jarring: chaotic

atoms: Dryden accepted the idea of the Greek philosopher Democritus (fifth century BC), who believed that all matter is made up of atoms

tuneful voice: the Word

cold, and hot, and moist, and dry: the contraries which make up the four elements (fire, air, water and earth)

stations: positions

compass: scale

diapason: octave cadence or concluding musical note

quell: calm

Jubal: in the Old Testament, 'the father of all such as handle the harp and organ' (Genesis 4: 21); the first musician

corded shell: a shell strung with dry sinews so as to become a musical instrument

brethren: brothers

celestial: heavenly

arms: weapons

shrill: high-pitched

dirge: funeral song

warbling: making a sound like water flowing gently downstream

frantic: wild, frenzied, highly excited

indignation: anger

wing: move upwards as though they had wings

mend: repair

Orpheus: the legendary pagan musician whose music was so powerful that he drew beasts and stones and trees after him when he played his lyre

Sequacious: compliant

vocal breath: suggesting the use of pipes and also the power of the organ to sustain notes like the human voice

straight: immediately

sacred lays: both the 'tuneful voice' that ordered the universe and the music of the spheres produced by cosmic harmony

crumbling pageant: the cosmos

devour: destroy

untune: harmoniously destroy; the power of harmony is now seen as going beyond the created world

'Alexander's Feast'

This work is subtitled 'The Power of Music; An Ode in Honour of St Cecilia's Day'.

Stanza 1
This stanza describes the greatness of Alexander, son of Philip of Macedon. The setting is a feast celebrating the defeat of Persia at the hands of Alexander's army. Alexander, a 'god-like hero', sits on his imperial throne with his brave peers gathered around him. Roses and myrtles decorate their heads. By his side sits the lovely Thais, in the full bloom of youth and beauty. 'Happy, happy, happy pair!' sings the poet. Only the brave deserves the fair. The chorus echoes his song.

Stanza 2
Timotheus the musician is sitting on high amid the choir. With flying fingers he touches his lyre and the trembling notes inspire heavenly joys. He sings of the divine origin of Alexander. Jove, the father of the gods in Greek and Roman mythology, is the real father of Alexander, sings Timotheus. For Jove fell in love with Olympia, Alexander's mother, assumed the disguise of a dragon, and made love to her. Thus he created an image of himself, a king of the world as Jove is king of the gods.

The listening crowd is awed by the song and looks upon Alexander as a god. Alexander, overcome by the fantasy of his own divinity, assumes the part and becomes convinced that his own nod, like Jove's, can shake the spheres. The chorus repeats the last five lines of the stanza.

Stanzas 3–4
Timotheus then sings in praise of the ever fair and young Bacchus, the god of wine and revelry who first ordained the joys of drinking. Wine is a rich treasure, and drinking is the sweet pleasure of the soldier. 'Sweet is pleasure after pain'. The chorus repeats the last lines of the stanza.

Soothed by the music, Alexander grows vain and thrice fights all his battles again in his mind. Timotheus the master, seeing the madness rise in Alexander's eyes, changes his song and checks the king's pride. His new song is a sad one, designed to create a mood of soft pity.

He sings of the fall of Darius, the Persian king, great and good but crushed by a severe fate and deserted and killed by his own followers. His slain body was left exposed on the bare earth, with not a single friend to close his eyes. The joy of victory evaporates from Alexander's soul, and he begins to contemplate the turns of fate in this life. Now and then he sighs, and finally his tears begin to flow. The chorus repeats the last four lines of the stanza.

Stanza 5
Pity prepares the mind for love, and love is the subject of Timotheus the mighty master's next song. War, he sings, is a constant, never-ending struggle and honour is empty. If the world is worth winning, then it is worth enjoying. The lovely Thais sits beside Alexander. Timotheus invites the king to take the good with which the gods have provided him.

The crowd applauds loudly, and Alexander, unable to conceal his pain, gazes at the fair lady and sighs many times. Finally, oppressed with wine and love, the 'vanquished victor' sinks upon Thais's breast. The chorus repeats the last seven lines of the stanza.

Stanza 6
Timotheus suddenly shifts the rhythm of his music to a louder strain, breaks the bands of Alexander's sleep, and rouses him to action. The king raises his head like a person awakened from the dead and stares around in amazement.

'Revenge!' cries Timotheus. See the Furies arise with flashing eyes and the snakes hissing in their hair. Behold a ghastly band of ghosts, each bearing a torch in his hand. These, sings Timotheus, are the ghosts of Grecian soldiers who were slain in battle and whose bodies remain unburied on the battlefield. The spirits cry out for vengeance and point their torches to the homes of the Persians and the temples of their gods.

The music fires Alexander and the princes with a zeal to destroy. Thais most of all is affected, and leads the king to burn the Persian city of Persepolis. In this, she is like Helen of Troy, whose passion for the Trojan prince Paris resulted in the Greeks burning Troy. The chorus repeats the last four lines of the stanza.

Stanza 7
This stanza shifts from the distant past to the present. Long ago, it tells us, before the invention of the organ, Timotheus with his flute and lyre was able to invoke in the human soul the entire scale of emotions, from rage to soft desire.

At last came the divine Cecilia, inventor of the organ. Inspired by God, she enlarged the former bounds of music by adding length to solemn sounds (through the organ's power to sustain notes).

Cecilia is superior to Timotheus, Dryden declares. Old Timotheus should yield the prize to her, or at least divide the crown. Timotheus succeeded in raising Alexander to the skies, creating in the king's mind the delusion of divine stature. But Cecilia's music succeeded in bringing an angel down from Heaven.

Grand Chorus
The poem ends with the Grand Chorus repeating the lines that concern St Cecilia. At last, we are told once again, divine Cecilia came, invented the organ, and enlarged the bounds of music by adding length to musical notes. Her music brought an angel down from Heaven, whereas Timotheus had previously succeeded only in creating the illusion of divinity in Alexander's mind. So Timotheus should yield the prize to Cecilia, or at least divide the crown with her.

NOTES AND GLOSSARY:

'Twas:	It was
Persia won:	Alexander the Great defeated Darius III, King of Persia, and captured the Persian city of Persepolis in 331BC
Philip's:	Philip of Macedon, father of Alexander
Aloft:	high
awful:	majestic
sate:	sat
valiant:	brave
peers:	equals; here, his generals
roses and . . . myrtles:	symbols of love and sensuality
desert in arms:	success in war
Thais:	the Athenian courtesan whom Alexander loved
Timotheus:	the mythical court musician of Alexander the Great
Jove:	in classical mythology, the father of the gods and god of thunder and lightning
belied:	disguised; that is, Jove disguised himself as a serpent and descended to earth
radiant spires:	shining coils
Olympia:	Olympias, Alexander's mother, claimed that Alexander's father was not Philip but a supernatural serpent; in the poem, Jove himself is presented by Timotheus as Alexander's father
sov'reign of the world:	Alexander; Timotheus is suggesting that Alexander, of divine origin, rules the world as Jove rules the gods
admire:	are awed by

vaulted:	arch-roofed
rebound:	echo
ravished:	delighted
Assumes the god:	Alexander submits to the fantasy of his own divinity and begins to behave as a god
shake the spheres:	when Jove nods, he shakes the universe; Alexander imagines that his own nod produces a similar result
Bacchus:	in classical mythology, the god of wine and revelry
ever:	always, forever
honest:	glorious
hautboys:	oboes (the oboe is a musical instrument that produces high notes)
breath:	that is, blow into them to create music
o'er:	over
thrice:	three times
master:	Timotheus
checked:	stopped
muse:	in classical mythology, the Muses were nine sister goddesses who presided over poetry and song; more generally, the goddess or the power regarded as inspiring a poet
infuse:	to introduce as by pouring; to imbue or inspire
Darius:	Darius III, the Persian king defeated by Alexander
welt'ring in his blood:	rolling and tossing in his blood (Darius was attacked by his own men)
utmost:	greatest
sate:	sat
Revolving:	pondering, thinking deeply about
'Twas but:	it required only
kindred:	closely related
Lydian:	soft
measures:	musical notes
rend:	tear
music won the cause:	that is, music has the power to control the imagination by directing the passions
vanquished:	defeated
horrid:	terrible, rough
awaked:	awakened
Furies:	in classical mythology, three female goddesses with snakes in their hair and terrible flashing eyes, who punished those guilty of unavenged murders;

here they invoke Alexander to avenge his unburied dead soldiers

ghastly band: terrible group

Grecian ghosts: the spirits of dead Greek soldiers

valiant: brave

abodes: homes

furious: intense

flambeau: torch

like another Helen, fired another Troy: Helen's passion for Paris (for whom she left her Greek husband King Menelaus) resulted in the Greeks besieging and burning the city of Troy; similarly, Thais's zeal leads Alexander to burn the palace of Persepolis

Ere: before

Cecilia: St Cecilia, patroness of music

vocal frame: organ

enthusiast: a person genuinely inspired by God

added length: the organ has the power to sustain notes

raised a mortal to the skies: created in Alexander's mind the delusion of divinity

drew an angel down: St Cecilia's holy music, it is told, actually attracted an angel down from heaven to earth

Part 3

Commentary

Absalom and Achitophel

Published in 1681, this poem is generally regarded as Dryden's major achievement and is also perhaps the best-known political poem in the English language. To understand it, and also to appreciate it to the full, we must first understand the political conflict with which it deals.

In 1678, England was shaken by fears of a Popish Plot to make Catholicism the religion of the country. An incredible liar called Titus Oates described the so-called Plot under oath. He insisted that he knew of a plan by Jesuits to murder King Charles and rule England as a Catholic state. Charles's legitimate successor, his brother James, was a Catholic and would, Oates claimed, serve as a puppet king under Jesuit control. The nation was swept by an almost unsurpassed sense of hysteria; other 'witnesses' supported Oates, trial followed trial, and many 'plotters' were subsequently put to death.

The Earl of Shaftesbury and his supporters, soon to be called the Whigs, hated James and used anti-Catholic feeling to try to block his succession to the throne. Indeed, the attempt to exclude James, Duke of York, from the English throne, was the major political consequence of the so-called Popish Plot. This was to be achieved by an Act of Exclusion, passed by Parliament. The aim of the Whigs was to replace James by Charles's illegitimate son, the Protestant Duke of Monmouth.

By 1681, belief in the existence of a Popish Plot was dying down, and a reaction took place in favour of royalism and James's succession. Shaftesbury was arrested, imprisoned and put on trial on a charge of high treason (he was later acquitted). It was at this point that Dryden published *Absalom and Achitophel*, supporting King Charles and his legitimate successor against Shaftesbury, Monmouth and their group.

Dryden's poem can be looked upon as the literary beginning of the Tory counter-attack against the Earl of Shaftesbury and his supporters, and as one of the most brilliantly written political poems in English literature.

The biblical base

For reasons which will be discussed later, Dryden rooted his poem in the Bible, in the story of Absalom's rebellion against his father, King David (II Samuel: 13–18). The parallel between Charles II and King David was commonplace in the writing of the time, and when Charles's illegitimate son Monmouth was suggested as successor to his father's throne, the parallel between Monmouth and Absalom became standard. Achitophel, Absalom's advisor in the Bible, was a well-known figure in the seventeenth century and was looked upon as a type of the evil politician. In 1627, for instance, a series of sermons was delivered at Oxford entitled *Achitophel: or the Picture of a Wicked Politician*.

Dryden's great originality lay not in associating the rebellion against Charles II with the earlier one against David in the Bible, but in developing this association at great length and in a highly skilful manner.

Dryden's use of conventional parallels from the Bible would have been immediately understood by a seventeenth-century reader. Today, however, these same parallels tend sometimes to frighten a student away from the poem. It is necessary, therefore, to make them very clear:

(1) King David=Charles II
(2) Absalom=Monmouth, Charles's illegitimate son
(3) Achitophel=Shaftesbury, in Dryden's poem the leader of the rebellion against Charles

In the Bible, it is, in point of fact, Absalom who leads the rebellion against King David. Achitophel appears only after Absalom has made his decision to rebel, and plays the secondary role of advisor. Dryden, however, was very aware of Charles's fondness for Monmouth, so he was careful to make Shaftesbury/Achitophel the principal figure in the rebellion while presenting Monmouth/Absalom as a pleasant but weak and ambitious person who yields to temptation.

While reading the poem, one should also keep in mind the following biblical parallels:

(1) Jerusalem=London
(2) Israel=England
(3) Jews=the Protestant English
(4) Jebusites=the Catholic English

52 · Commentary

The classical base

Absalom and Achitophel has often been referred to as a 'miniature epic',* for it contains most of the ingredients of an epic poem. The chief examples of epic poetry (also known as heroic poetry) are Homer's *The Iliad* and *The Odyssey*, and Virgil's *The Aeneid*. The major characteristics of an epic poem are the following:

(1) It recounts the great deeds of a central heroic figure, or group of figures. *The Odyssey*, for instance, tells how the Greek hero Odysseus, after many trials, returned to his native island and saved his wife and home from the suitors who wanted to disinherit him.
(2) It usually deals with a crisis in the history of a race or culture. Odysseus, for example, is a king, and his failure would have meant the collapse of his kingdom. The very concept of kingship is at stake in the poem, since his opponents wished to establish another form of government, an oligarchy or rule of the aristocratic few.
(3) It is written in an elevated, heroic style suitable to the subject matter. Verse, music and heightened diction are central features of the epic style.
(4) It is of great length.
(5) There is usually divine intervention. Odysseus, for example, is helped by the majority of the gods, but the god of the sea, Poseidon, is against him.

Although Dryden's poem lacks epic length, it does recount the great deeds of a central heroic figure, King David or Charles II. It also deals with a crisis in the history of ancient Israel or seventeenth-century England. The rebellion of Absalom and Achitophel is an attempt to undermine the legal authority of the king and to overthrow both human and divine order. In style, Dryden's poem is elevated and heroic, especially in the last section, when King David invokes the law and re-establishes order in his kingdom. Dryden, moreover, regarded satire as a species of heroic poetry, and *Absalom and Achitophel* is a satire. Finally, there is divine intervention in the poem. David is 'God's anointed', and God intervenes on his side in the end.

Thus *Absalom and Achitophel* is modelled on the Greek and Roman epics of Homer and Virgil; indeed it is possible to refer to it as an epic in miniature.

*Morris Freedman, 'Dryden's Miniature Epic', *Journal of English and German Philology*, Vol. LVII (1958), pp. 211–19.

Commentary · 53

Style

Absalom and Achitophel is, above all, a satire. Satire may be defined as a literary mode painting a distorted picture of part of the world in order to show its true moral nature. To illustrate this let us take an example from Homer's *Odyssey*. Circe, the enchantress, changes Odysseus's men into pigs in that epic because they made pigs of themselves while eating. Thus she reveals their true moral nature by distorting their physical appearance. What Circe did through magic, the satirist does in his writing. Dryden, by casting the Duke of Monmouth in the role of Absalom, King David's rebellious, illegitimate son, shows the real moral nature of Monmouth. And the same may be said, of course, of his presentation of the Earl of Shaftesbury as Achitophel, the type of the wicked politician.

Two kinds of satire were written by the Romans. On the one hand, there is Horace's urbane laughter at folly in familiar, witty language. On the other hand, there is Juvenal's indignant attack in sublime or lofty language upon vice. Both Horace and Juvenal were widely imitated in the sixteenth and seventeenth centuries by writers of moral verse satire. Dryden's clear preference was for Horace. Dryden's satire is witty and biting. His attack in *Absalom and Achitophel* upon Slingsby Bethel, for instance, one of the two Whig Sheriffs of London, cuts deep and excites the reader's urbane laughter. He portrays him as Shimei, who:

Did wisely from expensive sins refrain,
And never broke the sabbath, but for gain;

Shimei pretends to be religious, but Dryden exposes him satirically as a greedy lover of money. He refrains only from expensive sins (because they cost money) and never breaks the Sabbath unless there is money to be made out of so doing. Thus, Shimei uses religion to conceal his basic miserliness and obsession with the pursuit of wealth.

Absalom and Achitophel is written in heroic couplets, Dryden's favourite verse form and one which was widely used by the poets of the eighteenth century. The heroic couplet is a pair of rhyming iambic pentameter lines. Often, they encapsulate a basic idea. Here is an example:

The law shall still direct my peaceful sway,
And the same law teach rebels to obey;

This is King David speaking. Notice that each line is made up of five 'feet' or verse units, and that each 'foot' is made up of two iambic syllables; that is, the first syllable is lightly stressed, the second more strongly stressed. In the first line, for instance, the scansion is as follows:

Thĕ láw | shăll stíll | dĭréct | mў peáce | fŭl swáy |

The heroic couplet had been used earlier—by Shakespeare, (1564–1616), for instance, to terminate his sonnets—but it was Dryden who first used it extensively, as part of his attempt to reform and refine the English language. The heroic couplet, Dryden felt, brought order into poetry, restrained excesses, set limits, and got rid of discordant elements. Dryden assumed that the art of writing could be improved by the conscious application of principles, and the heroic couplet was one of his basic poetic principles. Alexander Pope had this to say of his distinguished predecessor: 'I learned versification wholly from Dryden . . . who had improved it much beyond any of our former poets; and would, probably, have brought it to its perfection, had he not been unhappily obliged to write so often in haste.'

Finally, the use of 'characters' in *Absalom and Achitophel* is a stylistic device that needs to be discussed. The writing of 'characters' was a widespread literary fashion in the seventeenth century. The 'character' is a word portrait of a type—a Lawyer, a Doctor, a Miser, a Puritan, a Jesuit, a Whig, a Tory. The classical precedent was the 'character' as written by Theophrastus (*c.*372–287BC).

Most 'characters' were denunciations, and were presented basically as deviations from Aristotle's (384–322BC) Golden Mean or middle way, but there was also a complementary school of exemplary 'characters'. Dryden gives us both types in *Absalom and Achitophel*, although his bad 'characters' are far more interesting and successful than his good ones. Further, he approximates each of his 'characters' to the portrait of an individual. And yet the individual's faults or virtues are made to suggest those of an entire class.

The most famous 'character' portrait in *Absalom and Achitophel* is Zimri, a satiric sketch of George Villiers (1628–87), the second Duke of Buckingham and one of King Charles's enemies. Buckingham as Zimri emerges as a man with an unbalanced mind:

Stiff in opinions, always in the wrong,
Was everything by starts and nothing long;
But in the course of one revolving moon
Was chemist, fiddler, statesman, and buffoon.

A ridiculous extremist who is unable to apply his mind steadily, Zimri is as inconstant as the moon. The word 'moon' also carries with it suggestions of lunacy.

Nor is Zimri capable of managing his financial affairs:

In squandering wealth was his peculiar art:
Nothing went unrewarded, but desert.

The overall picture, then, is of a mind that is unbalanced. Zimri's lunacy, however, is made by Dryden to suggest a quality shared by a large group of people. Zimri is a staunch supporter of Absalom and Achitophel. Through the use of the 'character' style, Dryden implies that no sane man would want his country to be ruled by such people: mental imbalance is a characteristic of the entire anti-Charles group.

Main ideas

There are two basic themes in *Absalom and Achitophel*. These are:

(1) The theory of sacred kingship, or the idea that kings are representatives of God on earth.
(2) The idea that history repeats itself. The rebellion against King Charles II is simply an instance of a rebellion which has occurred again and again in history. The reason why history moves in circles is that events are shaped by human nature, which is corrupt, having been itself shaped by Adam's initial act of disobedience.

The idea of sacred kingship marked a basic difference between Tories and Whigs in seventeenth-century England. The Tories believed that kingship was of divine origin, and that Adam had been the first monarch. After the Flood, Noah and his sons passed the rights of kingship to their descendants. The line of constituted kings, therefore, the Tories argued, was traceable to Noah and Adam. To interfere with it would be to destroy not only human but divine order. To the Tories, the Whigs were agents of chaos and even of Satan. The satanic Achitophel, when tempting Absalom to rebel, argues as follows:

'And nobler is a limited command,
Giv'n by the love of all your native land,
Than a successive title, long and dark,
Drawn from the mouldy rolls of Noah's Ark.'

In other words, Achitophel claims, an illegal king brought to power by the people is far superior to a legal successor whose basic claim to the throne stems from the musty rolls of Noah and his sons.

It is the Tory position of sacred kingship that Dryden adopts and defends so eloquently in *Absalom and Achitophel*. There are constant allusions in the poem to the alliance of kingship and divinity. David/

Charles is referred to as 'Israel's monarch, after Heaven's own heart'; he is 'God's anointed'; it is 'Heaven's decree', by Absalom's own admission, that James should be the legal successor; for the people to choose their own kings is to break 'At once divine and human laws'; and when David/Charles finally speaks, he is 'by heav'n inspired' and his judgement is supported by God with 'peals of thunder'.

The biblical parallel between Charles and David helped Dryden to solve one of his basic problems in writing *Absalom and Achitophel*. King David is a good example of a monarch who retained God's favour despite many transgressions, because of his importance to God's plans; and King Charles's many sexual lapses had to be condoned somehow. By drawing a parallel between the two kings, Dryden solved the problem and wrote the most eloquent of all his openings. Charles's sexual lapses are presented in a witty, forgiving manner that creates in the reader a mood of pleasant indulgence. This opens the way for David/Charles to speak as God's representative in the poem's last lines.

David/Charles is the real hero of *Absalom and Achitophel*, and is the only character who develops dramatically in the course of the poem. In the opening lines, he is boyish, a sexual adventurer, and over-indulgent towards Absalom. By the end, he has corrected these faults and assumed the full responsibility of divine kingship. Patient and merciful by nature, in the end he is forced to exercise his awesome authority and rout the rebels: 'Law they require, let law then show her face'. David/Charles invokes the law and restores order to his kingdom, defeating the agents of chaos.

This brings us to the second major theme of *Absalom and Achitophel*: the idea that history repeats itself. Human nature was shaped (but not determined, since we have free will) by Adam's initial act of disobedience. It is 'to sin' that 'our biassed nature leans', declares Dryden. Thus, the tendency to rebel against God's authority is strong in human beings. The first rebellion was that of Adam and Eve. Another significant example was the rebellion of Absalom and Achitophel against King David in the Old Testament. A third example is Monmouth's and Shaftesbury's revolt against King Charles. History abounds with other examples.

There is thus a very good reason why Dryden roots his poem in the Bible; for what better way to show the cyclical movement of history could there be than to demonstrate the similarities between the Old Testament rebellion against King David and the contemporary rebellion against King Charles II? The first rebellion foreshadows the second.

The greatest and most evil of rebels and tempters is Satan, and in drawing the character of Achitophel/Shaftesbury, Dryden deliberately associates him again and again with Satan. Achitophel/Shaftesbury is 'A name to all succeeding Ages cursed'. He is completely selfish, unprincipled and restless. Like Satan, his chief characteristics are treachery, hate and lust for power:

> In friendship false, implacable in hate;
> Resolved to ruin or to rule the state:

When he begins to tempt Absalom, using lies and promises of grandeur, he becomes most clearly a Satan-figure, whose venomous words remind us of the snake in the Garden of Eden. In attacking what amounts to a political paradise, he plays on Absalom's ambition and turns him against David/Charles.

If Achitophel is a Satan-figure, Absalom/Monmouth is an Adam-figure. As the poem begins, he is living in a sort of paradise, presided over by a kindly and indulgent father who has permitted him everything except succession to the throne. We are told of Absalom/Monmouth:

> Whate'er he did was done with so much ease,
> In him alone 'twas natural to please:
> His motions all accompanied with grace,
> And Paradise was opened in his face.

But Achitophel tempts him with the crown, the equivalent of the apple in the story of Adam and Eve. Unable to resist this temptation, Absalom/Monmouth reaches for the forbidden crown—and falls. His father is dismayed by this fall, but cannot prevent it and in the end is forced to punish it. Absalom/Monmouth, though by nature inclined to corruption, has had the free will to resist temptation, but has not done so. His story is a very familiar one.

Mac Flecknoe

If *Absalom and Achitophel* is Dryden's acknowledged masterpiece, *Mac Flecknoe* is his funniest and most delightful poem. Unfortunately it poses difficulties for the modern student, since it is packed with allusions, quotations and references, so the glossary in Part 2 is absolutely necessary to a full understanding of it. Once the many allusions are mastered, the student will find that it was well worth the time and effort.

Written perhaps as early as 1678, it was circulated in manuscript form until its publication in 1682. The occasion for the poem was a literary and personal quarrel between Dryden and Thomas Shadwell, a minor playwright of the period who saw himself as continuing Ben

Jonson's type of comedy. Although Dryden was himself a great admirer of Jonson, he did make some careful criticisms of his work, which prompted Shadwell to attack Dryden's own work. The final result of this literary quarrel between the two poets was *Mac Flecknoe*.

In *Mac Flecknoe*, Shadwell is presented not as a 'son' of Jonson (as he liked to think of himself) but as a 'son of Flecknoe' (which is what the title of the poem means). Flecknoe was a notoriously bad Irish poet who died in 1678. In the poem Dryden has him choose a successor in Shadwell, a person who will bring dullness and lack of wit to their triumphant culmination.

In style, *Mac Flecknoe* is a mock heroic satire written in heroic couplets. *Absalom and Achitophel* is also a satire in heroic couplets. The difference between the two poems is that Dryden in *Mac Flecknoe* uses the mock-heroic or mock-epic style. This is a literary mode where low or trivial subjects are treated in the high, artificial literary language of classical epic poetry. The point of the joke is to expose the silliness and ridiculous nature of the person or subject being satirised. By placing the mantle of the epic hero upon Shadwell or Sh—, Dryden reveals him for the complete fool that he considered him to be.

The following lines describing Sh—'s coronation are a good example of the mock-epic style:

The hoary Prince in majesty appeared,
High on a throne of his own labours reared.
At his right hand our young Ascanius sat,
Rome's other hope and pillar of the State.
His brows thick fogs, instead of glories, grace,
And lambent dullness played around his face.

The 'hoary [old] Prince' is Flecknoe, but the throne he sits on is a pile of his own ridiculous plays. Sh— is compared to Ascanius, Aeneas's son in Virgil's great Roman epic, the *Aeneid* (later translated by Dryden). But Ascanius's Rome in *Mac Flecknoe* is the capital of dullness. His brows are surrounded by thick fogs, and rays of dullness light up his face. The description is a clear parody of lines 930–2 in Book II of the *Aeneid*, where we are told that, from Ascanius's head 'A lambent flame arose, which gently spread/ Around his brows, and on his temples fed' (Dryden's translation). Dryden mockingly reveals the essential smallness and silliness of Flecknoe and Sh—by comparing the former to Aeneas and the latter to Ascanius. Elsewhere in the poem, moreover, Flecknoe is compared mockingly to the Roman emperor Augustus and Sh— to Romulus, one of the founders of the city of Rome.

Nor does Dryden stop there. Early in the poem, Flecknoe declares, addressing his son:

Heywood and Shirley were but types of thee,
Thou last great prophet of tautology.
Even I, a dunce of more renown than they,
Was sent before but to prepare thy way;
And coarsely clad in Norwich drugget came
To teach the nations in thy greater name.

Heywood, Shirley and, later in the poem, Dekker make up Dryden's list of bad dramatists from the preceding age. Here they represent Old Testament foreshadowings of Christ. Flecknoe, Dryden tells us, like John the Baptist, came out of the wilderness (Ireland) in coarse rags to prepare the way for the coming of Christ. Sh—, then, is the Word Incarnate, the 'last great prophet of tautology'. As a literary Christ he is the ultimate embodiment of dullness and lack of sense in literature. This comparison between Christ and Sh— is another example of Dryden's use of the mock-heroic style to expose the silliness of Shadwell.

The comparison is extended in the description of Shadwell's royal procession through the city of Augusta (London), which parodies Christ's triumphant entry into Jerusalem. Instead of the palm branches and garments that were spread in Christ's way, Sh—'s 'imperial way' is spread with the 'scattered limbs of mangled poets' and pages of the works of Heywood, Shirley and Ogilby, as well as of Sh— himself.

Flecknoe in the poem never pretends that his dullness is wit. On the contrary, he insists that he is the enemy of sense and wit, and that dullness is itself virtue. He chooses Shadwell to succeed him for the following reason:

The rest to some faint meaning make pretence,
But Sh—never deviates into sense.
Some beams of wit on other souls may fall,
Strike through and make a lucid interval,
But Sh—'s genuine night admits no ray,
His rising fogs prevail upon the day.

Flecknoe's ideal, then, is complete dullness, nonsense and lack of wit. It is because Shadwell embodies these qualities so completely that he is chosen by Flecknoe as his successor.

What is the main theme of *Mac Flecknoe*? Is the poem simply a hilarious attack on Thomas Shadwell undertaken for personal reasons, or is it more than that? Shadwell's solemn oath, during his coronation, hints at a more serious underlying message:

As Hannibal did to the altars come,
Sworn by his sire a mortal foe to Rome;
So Sh— swore, nor should his vow be vain,
That he till death true dullness would maintain,
And in his father's right and realm's defence
Ne'er to have peace with wit nor truce with sense.

The parallel between Sh— and Hannibal is, of course, mock-heroic; but there is also a deeper significance. When Hannibal was nine, he was forced by his father to swear enmity to Rome. When he grew up, he attacked and almost captured Rome in 216BC, thus proving to be one of its greatest enemies.

During the Augustan period, London was frequently compared to ancient Rome. Dryden strongly believed that the art of a nation is a measure of its health. He felt that people like Shadwell, if allowed to triumph in art, would create a cultural anarchy that could, in the end, lead to the downfall of London. So, in *Mac Flecknoe*, Dryden is attacking not simply Shadwell but the threat of dullness and cultural anarchy.

When Alexander Pope wrote *The Dunciad* some sixty years later, he gladly acknowledged that the basic plan of his great work on the vast force of dullness came from Dryden. Pope saw the threat of dullness as grimmer and greater than it had appeared to his predecessor. Dryden treats the threat briefly (*Mac Flecknoe* has 217 lines while *The Dunciad* is a huge work), but he is fundamentally quite as serious as Pope. One recent critic has observed of *Mac Flecknoe*: 'Dryden's placing of the action in the mercantile centre of London indicates the important and truly dangerous natural alliance he saw between Whigs, the mercantile middle classes, sedition, and bad art'.*

'A Song for St Cecilia's Day'

St Cecilia was traditionally the patroness of music and the inventor of the organ. The celebration of St Cecilia's Day on 22 November began in England in 1683, when the Musical Society commissioned annual odes from well-known poets and composers. The odes were usually written for musical performance and to celebrate the power of music. Dryden's two odes in praise of St Cecilia (the second, 'Alexander's Feast', was written ten years later in 1697) are both acknowledged to be masterpieces.

The ode is a poetic form that has a complex, formal stanzaic

*David Wykes, *A Preface to Dryden*, Longman, London, 1977, pp. 180–1.

pattern and that generally praises or celebrates one thing or person. Its content is primarily emotional and it is of medium length, for it cannot sustain a feeling of exaltation for a long time. The ode has its origins in Greek antiquity. At the turn of the sixth and fifth centuries BC the Greek poet Pindar wrote odes to praise the winners at the Olympic games. These Pindaric odes consisted of triads (groups of three sections each)—a strophe (or turn), an antistrophe (or counter-turn), and an epode (or stand). Their movement was through question and answer, or opposing statements, to a resolution. In seventeenth-century England, the Pindaric ode form was widely used in praise of music and poetry; such odes came to be known as musical odes. Dryden's two odes in praise of St Cecilia are musical odes in the full sense of the word, and were both set to music.

'A Song for St Cecilia's Day' is a masterly application of the doctrine of *rhythmus*, which Dryden defined in the Preface to his opera, *Albion and Albanius* (1685), as 'the choice of words', not 'elegancy of expression, but propriety of sound, to be varied according to the subject'. In other words, the poem 'imitates' emotions in its verse structure, and music should be used to emphasise this effect. The stanza on the flute and lute, for instance, captures in its choice of words the sad notes of those instruments, conveying this sadness to the reader or listener in the sound as well as the meaning:

> The soft complaining flute
> In dying notes discovers
> The woes of hopeless lovers,
> Whose dirge is whisper'd by the warbling lute.

The meaning here is captured through the sound by the use of a high incidence of long vowels and a very long fourth line following three short ones. Sound and subject reinforce and complete each other.

'A Song for St Cecilia's Day' is also interesting because in it Dryden presents the basic musical theories of his day. The poem has two major themes:

(1) The idea that the world was designed in harmonic intervals. This theory reconciles the music of the spheres with the Christian heavenly choir or the 'morning stars' that 'sang together' in the Old Testament (Job 38: 6–7), and is presented in the opening stanza and the conclusion of the 'Grand Chorus'.

The first stanza presents God as the archetypal musician. In the beginning, nature was a chaotic 'heap/ Of jarring atoms', but God's 'tuneful voice' composed these atoms into an ordered scale of being. The four elemental qualities—hot, moist, cold and dry—were assigned positions by the Almighty (referred to as 'Music') and formed a Chain of Being, each creature linked to every other in necessary sequence or 'compass of . . . notes'. Creation thus represents the fullest of harmonies, in which every possible note is heard, with Man as the concluding note. The first lines of this stanza, in accordance with the subject, lack rhyme and a distinguishable metrical pattern, while the final lines, which describe the harmony of the ordered universe, are beautifully composed, with both rhyme and rhythm.

The concluding lines of the ode, spoken by the 'Grand Chorus', refer to Judgement Day, when God shall 'untune' with the music of the trumpet the 'harmonious' universe whose spheres have been singing his praises. Paradoxically, the act of destruction is as harmonious as that of creation, for it is part of God's grand plan.

(2) The idea that music has the power to move its hearers and arouse in them varying emotions or states of the soul, with each instrument best suited to evoke a distinct emotion.

'What passion cannot music raise and quell!' exclaims Dryden, then demonstrates his statement in a series of brilliant stanzas. The trumpet and the drum excite us to martial passion, and drive us to arms. The flute and the violin excite in us various forms of erotic passion. But the organ is the noblest of all instruments, for its notes inspire 'holy love'. Thus, when Cecilia played her 'sacred organ':

> An angel heard and straight appeared
>   Mistaking earth for heav'n.

The stanzas on the effect of musical instruments (2–7) take the form of opposing statements. For instance, the drum, with its 'double double double beat', fevers the blood with a desire for battle, but is immediately followed by a stanza describing (and capturing) the soft, sad notes of the flute. Through these opposing statements, the ode moves to a kind of resolution. There is a progression from martial and erotic passion to holy love, to Cecilia and the organ. The first and last stanzas of the ode are also opposed, for one deals with the creation of the universe, the other with its destruction.

The student should keep in mind that the ideas about music expressed in 'A Song for St Cecilia's Day' were commonplace when Dryden wrote his poem in 1687. Dryden's great achievement was that he managed to express them with such force and vitality. His two Cecilia odes are triumphs of style rather than of original thinking.

'Alexander's Feast'

Written in 1697 and subtitled 'The Power of Music; An Ode in Honour of St Cecilia's Day', this work is generally preferred to Dryden's first Cecilia poem. 'Alexander's Feast' is a fine display of *rhythmus* (see above p. 61). Dryden chooses one of the greatest and most powerful figures in ancient history, Alexander the Great, and shows the influence that his court musician Timotheus is able to exert upon him. Using only one musical instrument, his lyre, Timotheus manages to move Alexander's emotions whichever way he wishes. Gradually, Timotheus emerges as the most important figure in the court, the master of the master of the world.

Dryden chooses his setting carefully—a feast celebrating Alexander's victory over the Persian king, Darius III, in 331BC. This was one of Alexander's greatest military triumphs, and Timotheus's musical triumph over him gains tremendous significance against such a background.

The ode is made up of seven stanzas. Each stanza describes and also *creates* an emotion, and each is followed by a chorus that embodies the emotional significance of the stanza. The emotions evoked in Alexander's soul by Timotheus's lyre in stanzas 2–6 are the following: the inspiration of divinity, bacchanalian joy, martial zeal, pity, love and revenge. But we must not forget that stanzas 1 and 7 also function to describe and create an emotion. The emotion embodied in the opening stanza is the joy of military victory, while stanza 7, with its hushed tone, evokes in us the emotion of religious devotion.

Dryden's verse is very ambitious in 'Alexander's Feast', as he swings from one extreme of violent emotion to the other. The rhythmical effects are daring and successful. In stanza 4, for example, Timotheus boldly melts Alexander's soul with pity for the defeated Darius:

> He sung Darius, great and good,
>   By too severe a fate
> Fallen, fallen, fallen, fallen,
>   Fallen from his high estate
> And welt'ring in his blood . . .

> With downcast looks the joyless victor sate,
>   Revolving in his altered soul
>   The various turns of chance below;
>   And now and then a sigh he stole,
>   And tears began to flow.

In the next stanza, Timotheus forces Alexander to sink upon the breast of his lovely mistress Thais, a 'vanquished victor'. But in stanza 6 he fires his soul and Thais's with a lust for revenge for the Grecian soldiers who died in battle against Darius and whose bodies remain unburied on the battlefield.

'Alexander's Feast', then, shows the power of Timotheus through his music to control the mind and soul of Alexander. And yet Timotheus as a musician is inferior to St Cecilia. The utmost he can achieve is to create in Alexander's mind the illusion of immortality. Cecilia, on the other hand, has succeeded in enlarging the former narrow bounds of music, and with her devotional music managed to draw an angel down from Heaven:

> Let old Timotheus yield the prize,
>   Or both divide the crown;
> He raised a mortal to the skies;
>   She drew an angel down.

To attract an angel from Heaven, Cecilia had to match the music of the spheres and the Christian heavenly choir. Thus she brought the full power of harmony to earth—the ultimate musical achievement. Timotheus, despite his excellence, is old, ancient and pagan. He has to yield the crown to the Christian Cecilia, or at best divide it with her.

The former Cecilia ode ended by contrasting Cecilia with the pagan Orpheus in stanza 7. Orpheus symbolised the power of music in traditional pagan mythology, but Cecilia is presented as superior to him, for she brought the full power of heavenly harmony to earth with her devotional music. 'Alexander's Feast' ends with a similar contrast between Timotheus and Cecilia, between pagan and Christian music.

Part 4

Hints for study

Approaching Dryden

The student of Dryden faces a seemingly enormous problem when he or she first confronts such poems as *Absalom and Achitophel* and *Mac Flecknoe*. The names are alien, the allusions seemingly impenetrable. Dryden's poetry, a student may hastily conclude, belongs to a different age, and to study it is a painful and tedious duty.

Nothing could be farther from the truth. There is some essential but basically simple background information that needs to be mastered before you can read and understand poems like *Absalom and Achitophel* and *Mac Flecknoe*. This background is given in the relevant sections of Part 2 and Part 3. Once it is absorbed, you will find that Dryden is one of the most delightful poets of the English language, and that it is easy to establish a lifelong friendship with him.

Here are some suggestions about how best to approach Dryden:

(1) In the case of *Absalom and Achitophel*, you should begin by acquainting yourself with the poem's political background and its biblical base, as explained in Parts 2 and 3. Until you understand who Absalom, Achitophel and King David are in the Old Testament, and until you absorb Charles II's problems with Monmouth and Shaftesbury in Dryden's age, it is not possible fully to appreciate the poem. This information is your key to understanding *Absalom and Achitophel*.

Once this key is in your hand, use it to enter directly into the delightful world of the poem. Refer to the glossary whenever necessary. The prose summary in Part 2 can be used in many ways, but beware of using it as a substitute for the excellent verse and sparkling wit of the poem itself. You might end by reading the critical commentary in Part 3, and then read the poem again.

(2) In the case of *Mac Flecknoe*, you should first familiarise yourself with its background—that is, the literary quarrel between Dryden and Thomas Shadwell. After that, you should read the

poem itself, but with constant reference to the glossary in Part 2. It is not possible to enjoy or understand the poem before you have mastered all the allusions in it. It may not be a bad idea also to use the prose summary at this stage.

Once you have understood the allusions in *Mac Flecknoe*, read it again. You will find that it is a wonderful and hilarious poem. After you have made this discovery, read the critical commentary in Part 3, then read the poem a third time.

(3) 'A Song for St Cecilia's Day' and 'Alexander's Feast' are musical odes that celebrate the power of music partly by creating a fusion of sound and subject. They are both stylistic masterpieces. Begin by reading them, preferably aloud. Then read the critical commentary in Part 3. This should provide you with insights into the poems. Read also the prose summaries in Part 2, paying particular attention to the glossary, for both poems contain allusions with which you should familiarise yourself. Finally, read the poems again. You will find that the relevant sections of Part 2 and Part 3 have deepened your understanding and enjoyment of them.

You should also guard against the feeling that Dryden's ideas are not relevant to our age. The idea, central to *Absalom and Achitophel*, that history moves in circles because human nature is corrupt and unchanging, is as old as the famous Greek historian Thucydides (c.460–c.400BC), and is widely accepted by historians today. Opposed to it is the idea that history moves in a straight line towards a specific goal—Communism in Marxist theory, for instance. Dryden's idea of sacred kingship in the same poem may be outmoded, but what prompted him to accept this idea was his deep consciousness of the fact that societies need a political system that will provide them with permanent stability and order. His solution to the problem may be unacceptable today, but he did manage to spotlight a major human concern. As long as the search for a political system that will ensure a permanent national and global peace continues, his outlining of the problem will remain of relevance to us.

As for *Mac Flecknoe*, it is a warning against dullness and cultural anarchy. Dryden in this poem advances the idea that the art of a nation is a mirror of its health. A nation that produces a large number of Flecknoes and Shadwells—and honours them—is in danger of collapsing. The two St Cecilia odes celebrate the power of music, and we all know how influential music in its various forms is today. Indeed, hardly a human society throughout history has failed to produce some sort of music. So Dryden's ideas are quite relevant today.

Extending your reading

Do not limit yourself to the poems discussed in these Notes. Be adventurous and extend your reading. It may be a good idea to read *Religio Laici* and *The Hind and the Panther*. Or you may wish to read something shorter like 'To the Pious Memory of the Accomplished Young Lady, Mrs Anne Killigrew' (1685). Allow yourself to be guided by your tastes and inclinations. If you have the time, read one or two of Dryden's plays. *All for Love* is his most famous play, but several others are very well-written and quite interesting. Formulate your own ideas about these works. Remember that examiners are always impressed by signs of independent thinking and reading.

Selecting central quotations

When you write about Dryden (or any other poet, for that matter), you are expected to back up your argument with a few central quotations. No one expects you to commit to memory large sections of Dryden, but if you can quote a couple of well-chosen lines every now and then, this will improve your essay greatly. Do not, however, simply quote lines in a parrot-like fashion. You should quote and *analyse* them.

Some examiners may test you by giving you a few lines from a Dryden poem and asking you to analyse them and perhaps draw some generalisations from them. The following are a few central quotations from the poems discussed in these Notes. In each case, (*a*) Identify the poem from which the quotation is taken; (*b*) Analyse the quotation in detail; (*c*) Connect one of the ideas or stylistic devices in the quotation to another idea or stylistic device you have come across elsewhere in Dryden. You will find that this is a valuable exercise that will help to train you in the close reading of poetry. Choose your own quotations, if you wish, and repeat this exercise with them:

(1) To change foundations, cast the frame anew,
     Is work for rebels who base ends pursue;
     At once divine and human laws control,
     And mend the parts by ruin of the whole.

(2) As Hannibal did to the altars come,
     Sworn by his sire a mortal foe to Rome;
     So Sh— swore, nor should his vow be vain,
     That he till death true dullness would maintain.

(3)   But when to sin our biassed nature leans
The careful devil is still at hand with means,
And providently pimps for ill desires:

(4)   What passion cannot music raise and quell!

(5)   Of these the false Achitophel was first:
A name to all succeeding Ages cursed. . .
In friendship false, implacable in hate;
Resolved to ruin or to rule the state.

(6)   'Heywood and Shirley were but types of thee,
Thou last great prophet of tautology.
Even I, a dunce of more renown than they,
Was sent before but to prepare thy way;'

(7)   So when the last and dreadful hour
This crumbling pageant shall devour,
The trumpet shall be heard on high,
The dead shall live, the living die,
And music shall untune the sky.

(8)   'Thou art my blood, where Jonson has no part;
What share have we in nature or in art?'

(9)   With ravished ears
The monarch hears,
Assumes the god,
Affects to nod,
And seems to shake the spheres.

(10)   Let old Timotheus yield the prize,
Or both divide the crown;
He raised a mortal to the skies;
She drew an angel down.

(11)   Railing and praising were his usual themes;
And both (to show his judgment) in extremes;

(12)   Shimei, whose youth did early promise bring
Of zeal to God and hatred to his King,
Did wisely from expensive sins refrain,
And never broke the sabbath but for gain;

(13)   'The law shall still direct my peaceful sway,
And the same law teach rebels to obey.' . . .
He said. Th' Almighty, nodding, gave consent,
And peals of thunder shook the firmament.

(14) 'The rest to some faint meaning make pretence,
But Sh—never deviates into sense.'

(15) Sharp violins proclaim
Their jealous pangs and desperation,
Fury, frantic indignation,
Depth of pains and height of passion,
    For the fair, disdainful dame.

Sample answers

Quotation 1: This quotation is obviously from *Absalom and Achitophel*. In it, Dryden attacks revolution and revolutionaries, claiming that they break (this is what the word 'control' means) both divine and human laws. To rebel is to break a divine law—thus, the theory of sacred kingship, which is central to the poem. Kings are representatives of God on earth. If a king makes mistakes, it is one's duty to help him find the correct path. To rebel against him, however, is to destroy the state. This idea can be connected to the Whig idea, expressed by Achitophel in the poem, that kings represent the people and can be changed by them when the need arises. The lines are in heroic couplets, which means that you should discuss this form of versification as part of your answer.

Quotation 2: The lines are from *Mac Flecknoe*. The scene is the coronation of Sh—. As part of the coronation, Sh— has to swear to his father, Flecknoe, that he will be a completely dull poet and playwright, and will never deviate from this course. The comparison with Hannibal is an example of the mock-heroic style that Dryden uses in this poem. The comparison serves to expose the silliness of Sh— by drawing a parallel between him and a truly great person. There is a serious side to the matter, though. As Hannibal was Rome's greatest enemy, so Sh—, if he were stronger, would be London's greatest enemy. Sh— represents 'dullness' in art, and the art of a nation is an index of its health. A strong, triumphant Sh— can destroy London. In *Absalom and Achitophel*, it is the Whigs and revolutionaries who pose a threat to the state; in *Mac Flecknoe* it is bad art. Your answer could also include an analysis of the heroic couplet form and a brief outline of the literary quarrel between Dryden and Shadwell.

Quotation 3: These lines explain Dryden's theory of human nature in *Absalom and Achitophel*. Because of the original disobedience of Adam and Eve, human nature is fallen and is biased towards sin.

We, however, have free will; although we are biased to sin, we are not predetermined in that direction. Satan is ever-active on earth to push us in the direction of sin and thus claim our souls. Your answer might well include an analysis of Absalom as an Adam-figure who is tempted by the satanic Achitophel, and yields after a struggle. It should also include an explanation of the heroic couplet form. The obvious link here is with Dryden's theory that history moves in circles; thus, the rebellion against Charles II is a repetition of the Old Testament rebellion against King David, which in itself repeats the rebellion of Adam and Eve.

Quotation 4: From 'A Song for St Cecilia's Day', this line celebrates the power of music to evoke various emotions in the human soul. The trumpet and the drum excite us to battle, while the flute evokes in us the emotion of hopeless love, and so on. The highest kind of music is that which St Cecilia played on her organ, devotional music that drew an angel down from Heaven. Dryden in this poem unites sound and subject as he describes the effect of each musical instrument, thus also creating the emotions he describes. The power of music is also celebrated in 'Alexander's Feast', where Timotheus with his lyre manages to control the emotions of Alexander the Great.

Essay questions

Most of the material for answering these questions can be found in the commentaries and notes on the poems, so guidelines are given after each question instead of an answer in essay form. The last question—on Dryden's deep love of order—is, however, given a full essay, partly because of its central role in his work and partly to offer the student a sample essay answer.

(1) Why does Dryden give *Absalom and Achitophel* a biblical base?

To answer this question, you might explain Dryden's circular view of history and his ideas about human nature. To what extent are we predestined by the original rebellion of Adam and Eve? To what extent do we have free will? Remember to support your argument with quotations and direct references to the text. Naturally, you will have to explain the rebellion of Absalom and Achitophel against King David in the Old Testament, and show how it parallels the rebellion of Monmouth and Shaftesbury against King Charles II, but remember that this is simply background information to your answer. The basic answer will stem from your detailed explanation of Dryden's ideas about history and human nature.

(2) Does *Mac Flecknoe* have a universal theme, or is it simply a hilarious personal attack on Thomas Shadwell?

The poem's universal theme is Dryden's attack on dullness and his fear of cultural anarchy. In *Absalom and Achitophel*, by contrast, the fear is of chaos and political anarchy.

(3) Discuss Dryden's views on democracy in *Absalom and Achitophel*.

This is a fascinating topic. The Greek philosopher Aristotle regarded democracy as the worst of all political systems, and Dryden fully agrees with him. Dryden accuses Shaftesbury of wanting Absalom as king so that the nation 'might be/Drawn to the dregs of a democracy'. The rule of the people was regarded by Dryden as an unstable and dangerous form of government. Can you defend democracy against this attack?

(4) Define an epic. To what extent does *Absalom and Achitophel* conform to the definition?

Begin by giving a full definition of the epic form, then give each major characteristic a separate paragraph, showing whether Dryden's poem embodies this characteristic or not.

(5) Trace the influence of Dryden on Alexander Pope.

This is a question that is often asked by examiners—if, that is, they have taught you Pope as well as Dryden. Pope inherited the heroic couplet form from Dryden, and his *Dunciad* is clearly influenced by *Mac Flecknoe*. The influence is deep and all-pervasive. This topic gives you a chance to exercise your own critical abilities.

(6) Discuss *Mac Flecknoe* as a mock-epic or mock-heroic poem.

An enjoyable topic. Be sure to support your argument with some quotations.

(7) Explain the theories of music advanced in 'A Song for St Cecilia's Day' and 'Alexander's Feast'.

Although the latter ode is often preferred to the former, the 'Song' offers a more complete statement of Dryden's ideas about music. It presents the idea that the world was designed in harmonic intervals, and that on the Judgement Day the sky will be 'untuned' by a musical instrument (the trumpet). The other idea is presented compactly in the line: 'What passion cannot music raise and quell!'

---

(8) Dr Samuel Johnson, the eighteenth-century critic, wrote: 'What was said of Rome adorned by Augustus may be applied by an easy metaphor to English poetry embellished by Dryden . . . he found it brick, and he left it marble'.

This is a vast topic that allows you to show your appreciation of Dryden. A knowledge of the poets that preceded Dryden, especially the Metaphysical poets, is necessary.

---

(9) Discuss Dryden's use of the 'character' portrait in *Absalom and Achitophel*.

The answer should begin with a definition of the 'character' portrait, then should examine 'characters' like Zimri, Shimei and others. At least one of the 'characters' loyal to King David should be analysed. Are there elements of the 'character' portrait in the presentation of David, Absalom and Achitophel?

---

(10) Dryden's major poetry exhibits a deep desire for order and a great fear of chaos. Discuss this characteristic as it manifests itself in the poems included in these Notes.

Dryden's deep love of order pervades his major poetry and manifests itself in different ways as we move from poem to poem.

Absalom and Achitophel is a search for permanent political stability in a world corrupted by original sin. It is 'to sin' that 'our biassed nature leans', and Satan is ever-present to lead us in that direction. Human beings have, however, the free will to reject Satan and embrace God. Dryden's love of order manifests itself in this poem in his vehement defence of the Tory theory of sacred kingship; he presents the clash between David/Charles, on the one hand, and Absalom/Monmouth and Achitophel/Shaftesbury, on the other, as a confrontation between God and Satan. In brief, the theory of sacred kingship holds that there is a succession of kings traceable in origin to Noah and his sons, and even to Adam. Adam and Noah were kings, according to this theory, and God's plan for the salvation of the human race requires that their sons inherit the kingship of various lands in unbroken succession. These kings represent God on earth. To rebel against them is a crime against human and divine law, and the result can only be chaos. When the satanic Achitophel tempts Absalom to rebel, he urges him to reject a succession derived from 'the mouldy rolls of Noah's Ark'.

This does not mean, of course, that a subject should offer his king blind obedience. Kings make mistakes, and it is the duty of a subject to help his king find the correct path. But to rebel is to sink the ship: it is an act of evil against God and man that has constantly tempted human beings throughout history. Dryden at the beginning of *Absalom and Achitophel* presents David/Charles as a boyish sexual transgressor, but he is 'God's anointed' and the poet's tone is pleasantly forgiving. By the poem's end, King David has matured, and he invokes the law and saves the state, with clear Divine aid and approval.

Absalom and Achitophel is written in heroic couplets, a verse form that reflects Dryden's deep love of order. The heroic couplet consists of two rhyming iambic pentameter lines that often encapsulate an idea. Here is an example from King David's concluding speech:

'How ill my fear they by my mercy scan;
Beware the fury of a patient man.'

Dryden believed that the heroic couplet restrained excesses and set limits, thus bringing order into poetry. It was his basic verse form, and one that he used extensively.

Mac Flecknoe is also written in heroic couplets, but apart from that, Dryden's love of order manifests itself in a different manner in this hilarious mock-epic poem. The poem is not simply an attack on Thomas Shadwell, who is presented as the favourite son of the notoriously bad Irish poet Flecknoe, but is also an attack on dullness and cultural anarchy. Flecknoe never pretends that he is witty; on the contrary, he insists that dullness is his cherished goal. During the coronation, Shadwell swears an oath:

As Hannibal did to the altars come,
Sworn by his sire a mortal foe to Rome;
So Sh— swore, nor should his vow be vain,
That he till death true dullness would maintain.

Shadwell swears that his art will always be the epitome of dullness. The comparison between Shadwell and Hannibal is clearly mock-heroic: Dryden places the mantle of greatness upon Shadwell to magnify his smallness and silliness. But the comparison also makes another point. Hannibal was Rome's greatest enemy, and Augustan London was often compared to ancient Rome. Dryden's idea is that, if Shadwell were strong enough, he would be able to destroy London with the weapon of dullness, spreading cultural anarchy throughout the land. It is no accident that the action of *Mac Flecknoe* takes place in the commercial centre of London, for Dryden regarded the commercial middle class as the enemy of true art. It is this class that allows people like Shadwell to flourish, and which may in the end undermine order and good taste in England.

In 'A Song for St Cecilia's Day' and 'Alexander's Feast', Dryden's love of order shows itself in his celebration of music. Music is itself rhythm and order; it is the enemy of chaos. The former poem presents the Word as 'a tuneful voice' that composed the universe, changing a chaotic 'heap/Of jarring atoms' into a 'harmonious', ordered scale of being. The style of the two poems, moreover, is itself a masterly celebration of order. Their stanzas, while describing various emotions, also create them in the language. The following lines, for example, not only describe the exciting martial beat of the drum, but also make us hear and feel this beat:

> The double double double beat
>   Of the thund'ring drum
>   Cries hark the foes come!
> Charge, charge, 'tis too late to retreat.

The drum-like effect is achieved through repetition, alliteration ('d' and 'b' in the first line, 'r' and 't' in the last), and the high incidence of short vowels.

Dryden's love of order, then, is all-pervasive. In *Absalom and Achitophel*, it reveals itself as a desire for permanent political stability; in *Mac Flecknoe*, it reappears in the attack on dullness and cultural anarchy; in the two St Cecilia odes, it shows itself as a deep love of music and harmony. In all these poems, the style is ordered and controlled, reflecting in linguistic practice this major theme of the verse.

Part 5

Suggestions for further reading

Dryden's works

James Kinsley's *Poems of John Dryden*, 4 volumes, Clarendon Press, Oxford, 1958, is the most comprehensive edition of Dryden's verse. The standard edition of Dryden's *Complete Works* has been issued by the University of California Press.

Biography

C. E. Ward's biography, published by the University of North Carolina Press in 1961, remains the most valuable work of its kind.

Criticism

There is a good deal of critical material on Dryden. The following four books are particularly useful for the non-specialist reader:

HARTH, PHILLIP: *Contexts of Dryden's Thought*, University of Chicago Press, Chicago, 1968. This book provides the student with the intellectual milieu of Dryden, placing him in the context of his period.

MINER, EARL: *Dryden's Poetry*, Indiana University Press, Bloomington, Indiana, 1971. A good, solid analysis of the verse.

WASSERMAN, GEORGE: *John Dryden*, Twayne Publishers, New York, 1964. A good introduction.

WYKES, DAVID: *A Preface to Dryden*, Longman, London, 1977. An excellent introduction to Dryden that studies him within his period.

The author of these notes

CHRISTOPHER S. NASSAAR was educated at the American University of Beirut, the University of Sussex and the University of Wisconsin. He has written on Rossetti and Wilde; his book *Into the Demon Universe: A Literary Exploration of Oscar Wilde* was published in 1974. He is also the author of the York Notes on Wilde's *The Importance of Being Earnest* and co-author of the York Notes on Shaw's *Candida*. At present, he is an associate professor of English and Cultural Studies at the American University of Beirut.

York Notes: list of titles

CHINUA ACHEBE
A Man of the People
Arrow of God
Things Fall Apart
EDWARD ALBEE
Who's Afraid of Virginia Woolf?
ELECHI AMADI
The Concubine
ANONYMOUS
Beowulf
Everyman
JOHN ARDEN
Serjeant Musgrave's Dance
AYI KWEI ARMAH
The Beautyful Ones Are Not Yet Born
W. H. AUDEN
Selected Poems
JANE AUSTEN
Emma
Mansfield Park
Northanger Abbey
Persuasion
Pride and Prejudice
Sense and Sensibility
HONORÉ DE BALZAC
Le Père Goriot
SAMUEL BECKETT
Waiting for Godot
SAUL BELLOW
Henderson, The Rain King
ARNOLD BENNETT
Anna of the Five Towns
WILLIAM BLAKE
Songs of Innocence, Songs of Experience
ROBERT BOLT
A Man For All Seasons
ANNE BRONTË
The Tenant of Wildfell Hall
CHARLOTTE BRONTË
Jane Eyre
EMILY BRONTË
Wuthering Heights
ROBERT BROWNING
Men and Women
JOHN BUCHAN
The Thirty-Nine Steps
JOHN BUNYAN
The Pilgrim's Progress
BYRON
Selected Poems
ALBERT CAMUS
L'Etranger (The Outsider)
GEOFFREY CHAUCER
Prologue to the Canterbury Tales
The Clerk's Tale
The Franklin's Tale
The Knight's Tale
The Merchant's Tale
The Miller's Tale
The Nun's Priest's Tale
The Pardoner's Tale
The Wife of Bath's Tale
Troilus and Criseyde
ANTON CHEKOV
The Cherry Orchard
SAMUEL TAYLOR COLERIDGE
Selected Poems

WILKIE COLLINS
The Moonstone
The Woman in White
SIR ARTHUR CONAN DOYLE
The Hound of the Baskervilles
WILLIAM CONGREVE
The Way of the World
JOSEPH CONRAD
Heart of Darkness
Lord Jim
Nostromo
The Secret Agent
Victory
Youth and *Typhoon*
STEPHEN CRANE
The Red Badge of Courage
BRUCE DAWE
Selected Poems
WALTER DE LA MARE
Selected Poems
DANIEL DEFOE
A Journal of the Plague Year
Moll Flanders
Robinson Crusoe
CHARLES DICKENS
A Tale of Two Cities
Bleak House
David Copperfield
Dombey and Son
Great Expectations
Hard Times
Little Dorrit
Nicholas Nickleby
Oliver Twist
Our Mutual Friend
The Pickwick Papers
EMILY DICKINSON
Selected Poems
JOHN DONNE
Selected Poems
THEODORE DREISER
Sister Carrie
GEORGE ELIOT
Adam Bede
Middlemarch
Silas Marner
The Mill on the Floss
T. S. ELIOT
Four Quartets
Murder in the Cathedral
Selected Poems
The Cocktail Party
The Waste Land
J. G. FARRELL
The Siege of Krishnapur
GEORGE FARQUHAR
The Beaux Stratagem
WILLIAM FAULKNER
Absalom, Absalom!
As I Lay Dying
Go Down, Moses
The Sound and the Fury
HENRY FIELDING
Joseph Andrews
Tom Jones
F. SCOTT FITZGERALD
Tender is the Night
The Great Gatsby

E. M. FORSTER
A Passage to India
Howards End

ATHOL FUGARD
Selected Plays

JOHN GALSWORTHY
Strife

MRS GASKELL
North and South

WILLIAM GOLDING
Lord of the Flies
The Inheritors
The Spire

OLIVER GOLDSMITH
She Stoops to Conquer
The Vicar of Wakefield

ROBERT GRAVES
Goodbye to All That

GRAHAM GREENE
Brighton Rock
The Heart of the Matter
The Power and the Glory

THOMAS HARDY
Far from the Madding Crowd
Jude the Obscure
Selected Poems
Tess of the D'Urbervilles
The Mayor of Casterbridge
The Return of the Native
The Trumpet Major
The Woodlanders
Under the Greenwood Tree

L. P. HARTLEY
The Go-Between
The Shrimp and the Anemone

NATHANIEL HAWTHORNE
The Scarlet Letter

SEAMUS HEANEY
Selected Poems

JOSEPH HELLER
Catch-22

ERNEST HEMINGWAY
A Farewell to Arms
For Whom the Bell Tolls
The African Stories
The Old Man and the Sea

GEORGE HERBERT
Selected Poems

HERMANN HESSE
Steppenwolf

BARRY HINES
Kes

HOMER
The Iliad
The Odyssey

ANTHONY HOPE
The Prisoner of Zenda

GERARD MANLEY HOPKINS
Selected Poems

WILLIAM DEAN HOWELLS
The Rise of Silas Lapham

RICHARD HUGHES
A High Wind in Jamaica

THOMAS HUGHES
Tom Brown's Schooldays

ALDOUS HUXLEY
Brave New World

HENRIK IBSEN
A Doll's House
Ghosts
Hedda Gabler

HENRY JAMES
Daisy Miller
The Ambassadors
The Europeans
The Portrait of a Lady
The Turn of the Screw
Washington Square

SAMUEL JOHNSON
Rasselas

BEN JONSON
The Alchemist
Volpone

JAMES JOYCE
A Portrait of the Artist as a Young Man
Dubliners

JOHN KEATS
Selected Poems

RUDYARD KIPLING
Kim

D. H. LAWRENCE
Sons and Lovers
The Rainbow
Women in Love

CAMARA LAYE
L'Enfant Noir

HARPER LEE
To Kill a Mocking-Bird

LAURIE LEE
Cider with Rosie

THOMAS MANN
Tonio Kröger

CHRISTOPHER MARLOWE
Doctor Faustus
Edward II

ANDREW MARVELL
Selected Poems

W. SOMERSET MAUGHAM
Of Human Bondage
Selected Short Stories

GAVIN MAXWELL
Ring of Bright Water

J. MEADE FALKNER
Moonfleet

HERMAN MELVILLE
Billy Budd
Moby Dick

THOMAS MIDDLETON
Women Beware Women

THOMAS MIDDLETON *and* WILLIAM ROWLEY
The Changeling

ARTHUR MILLER
Death of a Salesman
The Crucible

JOHN MILTON
Paradise Lost I & II
Paradise Lost IV & IX
Selected Poems

V. S. NAIPAUL
A House for Mr Biswas

SEAN O'CASEY
Juno and the Paycock
The Shadow of a Gunman

GABRIEL OKARA
The Voice

EUGENE O'NEILL
Mourning Becomes Electra

GEORGE ORWELL
Animal Farm
Nineteen Eighty-four

JOHN OSBORNE
Look Back in Anger

WILFRED OWEN
Selected Poems

ALAN PATON
Cry, The Beloved Country

THOMAS LOVE PEACOCK
Nightmare Abbey and *Crotchet Castle*

HAROLD PINTER
The Birthday Party
The Caretaker

PLATO
The Republic

ALEXANDER POPE
Selected Poems

THOMAS PYNCHON
The Crying of Lot 49

SIR WALTER SCOTT
Ivanhoe
Quentin Durward
The Heart of Midlothian
Waverley

PETER SHAFFER
The Royal Hunt of the Sun

WILLIAM SHAKESPEARE
A Midsummer Night's Dream
Antony and Cleopatra
As You Like It
Coriolanus
Cymbeline
Hamlet
Henry IV Part I
Henry IV Part II
Henry V
Julius Caesar
King Lear
Love's Labour Lost
Macbeth
Measure for Measure
Much Ado About Nothing
Othello
Richard II
Richard III
Romeo and Juliet
Sonnets
The Merchant of Venice
The Taming of the Shrew
The Tempest
The Winter's Tale
Troilus and Cressida
Twelfth Night
The Two Gentlemen of Verona

GEORGE BERNARD SHAW
Androcles and the Lion
Arms and the Man
Caesar and Cleopatra
Candida
Major Barbara
Pygmalion
Saint Joan
The Devil's Disciple

MARY SHELLEY
Frankenstein

PERCY BYSSHE SHELLEY
Selected Poems

RICHARD BRINSLEY SHERIDAN
The School for Scandal
The Rivals

WOLE SOYINKA
The Lion and the Jewel
The Road
Three Shorts Plays

EDMUND SPENSER
The Faerie Queene (Book I)

JOHN STEINBECK
Of Mice and Men
The Grapes of Wrath
The Pearl

LAURENCE STERNE
A Sentimental Journey
Tristram Shandy

ROBERT LOUIS STEVENSON
Kidnapped
Treasure Island
Dr Jekyll and Mr Hyde

TOM STOPPARD
Professional Foul
Rosencrantz and Guildenstern are Dead

JONATHAN SWIFT
Gulliver's Travels

JOHN MILLINGTON SYNGE
The Playboy of the Western World

TENNYSON
Selected Poems

W. M. THACKERAY
Vanity Fair

DYLAN THOMAS
Under Milk Wood

EDWARD THOMAS
Selected Poems

FLORA THOMPSON
Lark Rise to Candleford

J. R. R. TOLKIEN
The Hobbit
The Lord of the Rings

CYRIL TOURNEUR
The Revenger's Tragedy

ANTHONY TROLLOPE
Barchester Towers

MARK TWAIN
Huckleberry Finn
Tom Sawyer

JOHN VANBRUGH
The Relapse

VIRGIL
The Aeneid

VOLTAIRE
Candide

EVELYN WAUGH
Decline and Fall
A Handful of Dust

JOHN WEBSTER
The Duchess of Malfi
The White Devil

H. G. WELLS
The History of Mr Polly
The Invisible Man
The War of the Worlds

ARNOLD WESKER
Chips with Everything
Roots

PATRICK WHITE
Voss

OSCAR WILDE
The Importance of Being Earnest

TENNESSEE WILLIAMS
The Glass Menagerie

VIRGINIA WOOLF
Mrs Dalloway
To the Lighthouse

WILLIAM WORDSWORTH
Selected Poems

WILLIAM WYCHERLEY
The Country Wife

W. B. YEATS
Selected Poems